© Nancy Knudsen 2016. All rights reserved.

Without limiting the rights under copyright reserved above, no part of this publication may be reproduced, stored in or introduced into a retrieval system, or transmitted in any form or by any means (including but not limited to electronic, mechanical, photocopying, or recording), without the prior written permission of the copyright owner.

ISBN: 978-0-9945093-0-7

Editor: Diana Giese
Designer: Audrey Larsen, compu-vision
Printed by Dennis Jones and Associates Pty Ltd

Published by Tamejin Publishing Australia
2 Barrack Street, Sydney, 2000

Accidentally Istanbul

Nancy Knudsen

Contents

1. Into the unknown 1
2. Arrival in Istanbul 8
3. On the doorstep 12
4. Osman 19
5. Getting to know you 27
6. Istiklal Caddesi 37
7. Work—and an accident. 43
8. Life on crutches. 48
9. A Turkish friendship 55
10. The fruit of the land 59
11. Teaching in Istanbul 70
12. Claudia's foodie walk. 78
13. The Bosphorus 92
14. Refugees of Turkey 100
15. Headscarves. 110
16. The multipurpose repairman 123

17	Turkish eyes	133
18	Ramazan	138
19	Getting a visa	143
20	Falling under the spell	161
21	Guests	164
22	Rogues, thieves and drivers	169
23	Dogs that own themselves	174
24	Feasts and festivals	181
25	Staying longer	187
26	Winter white	192
27	Visitors	198
28	Ebru	206
29	The test	212
30	Dilemmas	222
	Epilogue	231

My father said many years ago: 'When the time is right, you will know, you will feel it in the air. There will be no decision to make; the road will appear like magic in front of you.'

The time is right now. This is a story I have to tell, to set to rights some wrongs—maybe for myself, maybe for others too.

1

Into the unknown

'You want to do *what*? Get off the boat? Are you crazy?' I couldn't believe what my husband Ted, normally so sane and dependable, was saying. 'We're in the middle of a sailing holiday. You don't just *get off* the boat. And we'd planned to do this—for years. We're nowhere near finished …'

He looked a little shocked at my vehemence. 'It's only for the winter. Our summer sailing is almost over.'

I could feel my breaths coming short and fast. 'They want you to teach architecture in their university? In Istanbul? For a whole semester? I can't believe they're serious. You've never been a teacher, let alone a university lecturer. You don't have the slightest interest in academic life. Why start now?'

I paused and then produced my trump card. 'And you can't speak the language.'

Accidentally Istanbul

We were sitting in the saloon of our comfortable cruising boat, Ted at the chart table where he had just taken the fatal phone call, while I perched tensely on the companionway. He was still staring at the phone as if it might suddenly spring to life.

'Well ...' he said, screwing up his nose, 'It might be interesting.'

'Interesting? *Interesting? No no no no!* We came here to sail— not to go gallivanting off somewhere on land. We can spend time with Turkish people right here in the sunshine.'

Ted grinned. 'They're still Turkish up there in Istanbul.'

'But, but—' I didn't want to say the words that were forming in my mouth: *They're Muslim, proper Muslims up there. We don't know what that would be like.* I moderated this. 'And they'll be *city* people, not like the friendly villagers here in the south.' While sailing around Turkey we had found the people in small coastal villages most hospitable.

'Where's your sense of adventure? The University has invited us there for two days. Let's go and see what it's like.'

No no no no no ... The screaming filled my mind. *This is not happening. Istanbul, for the winter? It will not only be freezing but claustrophobic, surrounded by people who pray five times a day. He'll hate teaching, I know it—but by then we'll be trapped.*

Thinking quickly, I decided to be persuasive. 'If you want to move on, we could extend the summer a little. Sail on to Greece, Croatia. The winds would be with us ...'

Accidentally Istanbul

I was simply not going to let this happen. I could feel my metaphorical jaw setting firm. This was an argument *I was going to win*.

• • •

It's a one-hour flight from the small coastal town of Finike, where we left the boat, to Ataturk Airport in Istanbul. With a glass of white wine in my hand, gazing out the window at a vast, clear blue sky and below us square green fields, I had time to reflect on just how I had given in and was now on this aircraft.

Ted and I had been sailing the coastline of southern Turkey during the three-week stay we had planned. It was 2005. Good friends, Malcolm and Carolyn, were with us. We swam in clear, shark-free water, wandered the countryside, ate simple, enticing Turkish food and woke to the sound of lapping waters and crowing roosters on the hills. Life had become bubbly with laughter, languorous.

In warm, gentle weather we had sailed into the tiny 22 Fathom Bay, surrounded by high tree-covered mountains. The water was too deep for anchoring, so our boat was tied with others to the wharf. A farm, a tumbledown stone building and outhouses, stretched up the hillside. A scattering of goats and donkeys, chickens and geese grazed the sparse grass. The sunshine hung heavily, insects flitting, buzzing, a chorus in the air.

A family, elderly mother and daughter, always in brown or

Accidentally Istanbul

beige headscarfs, ran an eight-seat 'restaurant' with a brother. It was merely an iron roof held up by a trellis covered in twisted, thick-trunked vines. Fat bunches of grapes hung down towards the rough wooden table and there were no walls. The family ran down the hill from their house carrying each course. The food was superb: fresh grilled fish, home-grown vegetables.

One evening at the shore we were in swimmers and sarongs, draped messily in towels, hair wetly plastered, cheeks reddened by the sun. Malcolm and Carolyn chatted to some young men on the wharf beside their tender.

I was still up the hill talking to some other yachties. We had just arranged dinner under the trellis, at seven. Through the flow of the conversation, I could sense that there were two people approaching me. Carolyn was walking up from the wharf, and the daughter was running down the hill towards me.

Carolyn reached me first. 'We've met these really lovely Turkish people from that *gulet* over there,' she said, pointing to a traditional Turkish sailing boat for tourists. 'They've invited us for a drink.'

'Lovely,' I said, watching the daughter running towards us, 'but it's already six and dinner is at seven. We don't have time if we're going to shower and change.'

'You're right. I'll go and explain.' Carolyn turned and went back to the wharf.

The daughter was still running, and getting closer. Malcolm knelt to help undo the lines connecting the young men's dinghy

Accidentally Istanbul

to the wharf. Carolyn stood back and gave them a small wave just as the daughter arrived at my side, panting.

'My brother, he just rang me. Can you come later for dinner, because he is delayed a little with the fish? Perhaps 8.30pm?'

Maybe we could have that drink with Carolyn's new friends after all.

I turned and started to head down to the wharf. But too late. The young men's dinghy had already left. *Doesn't matter*, I thought. But I told Carolyn and she gave them another wave. *They probably won't see her*, I thought. By the merest chance they did. That one small glance backward was to change our lives.

They stopped their dinghy engine to listen and when they heard of our change of plans, they immediately returned to the wharf to pick us up.

On the chartered *gulet* we found around 30 holiday-makers. They were, we learned, the staff and President of an Istanbul university. We spent a delightful couple of hours swapping stories. Ted the architect was in his element, telling unlikely (but almost true) stories of life and tales of building skyscrapers in the Antipodes. Soon the entire party was gathered around us, lying on cushions on the deck or propped against the mast, laughing. We drank apple tea while Ted spoke of Australian architectural styles and how we much we were enjoying sailing in Turkish waters.

Then, just like that, we were invited to Istanbul to be their guests 'any time'. Arrangements were made to host Malcolm and

Accidentally Istanbul

Carolyn when they passed through the city on their way back to Australia. Ted was invited to join their Faculty of Architecture. He accepted with a careless laugh, he and the President shaking hands to much accompanying applause. In our turn we invited them all to billy-tea (with the essential gumleaf) in Australia. They all accepted, too.

When they left the anchorage they tooted their horn in farewell and as far as we were concerned, this simply marked the end of a very pleasant encounter.

But what we had both dismissed as an amusing idea at a social meeting, merely a joke, was now coming to pass.

While I ran over this on the plane, my stomach churned. I dozed uncomfortably, starting with a jerk every time the engines made a different sound. I knew practically nothing of Islam. How much would I be drawn, against my inclination, into a strange new Muslim world?

Every time I glanced at Ted he was reading placidly. 'That's men for you,' I told myself. 'No reflection.'

I had spent half a lifetime in the travel industry and was an experienced traveller. But no one had ever expected me to join in the everyday lives of the people of the countries I visited—as a resident, not a traveller merely passing through. My mind was going wild with possibilities. Would living in Istanbul mean feeling obliged to attend a mosque sometimes to be polite, just as people at home felt 'obliged' to attend church at Christmas?

Yes, I concluded, I was on this plane because I really did adore

Accidentally Istanbul

my husband and best friend Ted. I wanted him to be happy—but I feared our dream sailing holiday might end up turning into a nightmare.

2

Arrival in Istanbul

The front door, polished wood and brass knocker, was slightly ajar. I reached out and hesitantly pushed it. Beyond was a small marble hallway, almost immediately filled with several swarthy, moustachioed faces. A crowd of grinning, stocky men with vacuum cleaners and cleaning cloths peered at us. One held out his arms in an expansive gesture, his fat middle shaking as he flailed a dusting cloth. He let fire a blast of rapid Turkish, beaming under his thick moustache. The scene was both comical and vaguely alarming.

Before we had time to react we were joined by the blue-eyed young driver who had chauffeured us, in silent amusement, from Istanbul Airport. He spoke no English but during the journey had sporadically twisted in his seat, nodding and smiling.

'What do you think he finds so funny?' I had muttered to

Accidentally Istanbul

Ted. We were being whisked across the city, our hands clutched together. The greeting at the airport had been strange: wide smiles, lots of help with our luggage, but not a word of English.

'No idea—but I'd like to know where we're actually going. Look up "where" in the dictionary.'

'Maybe our driver isn't from the University at all,' I suggested. 'Maybe he's a white slave-trader.' But I reached into my bag for my tiny dictionary and looked up the word. '*Nerede*. Or *nereye*. Or *nerele*. It gives all three.'

Ted leant forward towards the driver. '*Nerede, nereye, nerele?*' he asked with a smile of his own. The driver was actually laughing while he answered, which masked his words a little, as he twisted dangerously again to look at us.

'What did he say?' whispered Ted.

'Sounded like Attila.'

'Attila? He was a Hun, not a Turk.' He started chuckling.

'Attila, Attila.' The driver was nodding agreement. As he drove on he continued to twist round in his seat to grin.

'Don't ask him any more questions—please! He'll run us off the road.'

We arrived frazzled but safe. Having greeted the cleaning brigade, our driver loped back to the luggage-filled lift and, with the bumbling but enthusiastic help of some of the cleaners, started to heave our cases into the flat.

We stepped forward.

Around the corner in a flood of light was a living room with

Accidentally Istanbul

wide windows. A torrent of lacy white curtains framed the view over a sports stadium. I looked around. Apart from the sunshine streaming into the room, it looked to be in mourning. Nearly all the furniture was black. There was a glass and wrought-iron dining table with narrow-backed black leather chairs, a black leather couch and two lounge chairs, an almost-black marble sideboard and smoky mirrored walls. The room had considerable pretensions to grandeur, but all that blackness made it oddly dispiriting.

I retreated down the hall. There was a kitchen on the left giving an impression of whiteness with a strong smell of bleach. Then one, two, three bedrooms, with thick carpets, also black, shiny ebony furniture, many mirrors and a whiff of damp. The ceilings were extraordinarily elaborate. I stood for a moment gasping at the intricacy of them, my Australian eyes disconcerted by such flamboyance.

'Ted! Look at this ceiling.' He is always fascinated by design. He stared, uttered an expletive, and wandered away. Well, what did I expect of a self-declared minimalist architect?

There was only one bathroom but it was large, with a marbled floor, a carved (black) marble vanity and more odour of bleach. After my many forebodings, I breathed easier. This was certainly not how I would furnish an apartment—*one wouldn't want to encourage suicidal tendencies*—but it was comfortable enough for a winter in Istanbul.

A vast unknown stretched before me, before us. Ted was

Accidentally Istanbul

on an erratic high, excited as a child. But I couldn't begin to imagine how our sojourn in this completely strange Muslim city would turn out for us. I comforted myself that it was only for a few months, a single semester.

3

On the doorstep

As I wandered from room to room, I still found it hard to believe I was in Istanbul.

Since we had met and married some years before, Ted Nobbs and I had lived the stressed-out life of busy professionals in inner-city Sydney. Some months before, we had fled everything familiar to us to bring some light and laughter, some hedonism into our lives. We deserved it, I had convinced myself, and had led our flight.

Ted had often expressed regret that we spent so little time together. I had been 25 years in my latest career and Ted had practised architecture for even longer. Often I found myself wondering: *Is our life merely to be this consumption-oriented, brand-led, competitively aimless world of traffic snarls and graffiti?* I yearned for something better that I couldn't name. Not that

Accidentally Istanbul

I hadn't wanted the executive life, yearned for it, seen it as the pinnacle of achievement. But increasingly what I called *my life* felt like a chain around my neck.

I had grown up in Queensland and saw Sydney as a heady confection of fun and sophistication. I craved its high energy, power and privilege, and regarded it as a place where every breath signalled exhilaration and opportunity. I had longed to be part of that. As a woman who did well in business, every time I had a win I felt that I was winning for all women. I also loved the opportunities I was able to give others.

Yet finally, without quite understanding how, I felt like the boy who saw that the emperor was not wearing any clothes. In a kind of second adolescence, I began to ask: *What is life all about?* Why, when it had been so kind to me, with a husband I loved, two beautiful grown-up children, challenging work and an enviable lifestyle, was I dissatisfied?

Leaving the workforce had been a momentous and frightening escape. Now, even more suddenly, we were giving up our barely-developed new leisure life. This was a new challenge for Ted in an exotic location—but what about me? After my initial strongly negative reaction, I had given in quite quickly. *It's only for the winter ... only for the winter*, the words were a mantra in my head. But how would I fill my time? Sightseeing would last a little while—but after that? Could I also find a job? Was that even possible? And what would I do? No answers hung in the air before me. Were we simply proving that our fate was the grind

Accidentally Istanbul

of daily work, attracted to it instinctively, like moths to a flame?

But now we were committed. The worst part was telling friends and family by telephone that our planned three-week sailing holiday in Turkey had morphed into working life in Istanbul for Ted—and who knew what for me—until the European spring.

This had been late summer 2004, with the events of 9/11 in New York in 2001 still fresh in our minds. The world was becoming troubled in new and terrifying ways. Islamophobia was not a term that had yet come into common use—but it soon would.

'Turkey? But isn't that a Muslim country?' one friend asked, implying foolhardiness.

'It's all very well to *visit* Turkey,' another friend told Ted. 'I've been there, and it's beautiful. But to *stay* there? The Middle East is dangerous these days, you know.'

'Istanbul for the winter? What about all those Muslims?' commented others.

These misgivings shook me. 'Well, I don't know any Muslims yet—not really,' I countered defensively. 'Do you think it might actually be dangerous?'

'I wouldn't feel safe among Arabs.'

At this I felt a rush of irritation. 'Actually, they're not Arabs.' We had learned enough to know Turkish people had different backgrounds.

In spite of my university education, up until then I had little

Accidentally Istanbul

knowledge of Turkey and its people—and little interest. Ted, having gone directly from school to the study of architecture, knew a lot about the history of art, but as little as I about world history. While he didn't show the slightest embarrassment, I was disconcerted by the fact that Turkish people seemed to know much more about us than we did about them.

While sailing, we had met an eclectic collection in the villages we visited, some of whom we had befriended. But we had come to Turkey with nothing more demanding than fun on our minds. We had simply wanted time out to sail and swim, to enjoy the food and local wine.

We found, however, that the English-speaking Turkish people we met were all anxious to educate us about their country and vitally interested in discussing its culture, history and future. They wanted us to share their passions, and we engaged in lengthy conversations, sometimes intensely one-sided. They described the troubled area of the Arab Middle East as backward, lacking in democracy and struggling with religious fundamentalism. By contrast, they prided themselves on the gap they filled between West and East.

But I was still disconcerted by the misgivings from home. In truth I would have gone for a vacation in Hell if I thought it would make Ted happy. But in private moments, I continued to feel sharp stabbings of trepidation.

What would everyday life be like in such a large Muslim city? We would not have diplomatic immunity, or be expats with the

Accidentally Istanbul

protection of an employing corporation. Would the fact that we were, while not religious, born of a Christian culture make a difference once we were no longer tourists or guests but foreign interlopers?

I strove to conquer my anxiety, but the questions kept slinking in when my metaphorical back was turned.

I thought that starting to read about the place and its culture might light up my dark tunnels of ignorance. After reading the Lonely Planet guide, I bought a biography of Ataturk, the Father, the first leader, of modern Turkey.

Why did both Ted and I know so little? In geography at school all I could remember being taught was that Turkey, 'Asia Minor', was a land shaped like a flat scone, which didn't fit (irritatingly) into either Europe or Asia. It straddled both, showing the sort of geographical indecision which didn't please our geography teacher.

In history classes, fighting yawns, we had memorised the dates of the reigns of the Kings and Queens of England and their victorious battles. We also learned a little about Europe— Napoleon, the Tsars—but absolutely nothing, zip, zero, about Turkey.

We had a lot of catching-up to do.

I started reading at a furious pace. I read how Istanbul had begun as a small city-state not much bigger in area than today's Palace of Topkapi in the old city, but so cleverly situated, with the shimmering Sea of Marmara on one side and the

Accidentally Istanbul

placid Golden Horn on the other, that it was easy to defend. Over the centuries, as the city known as Byzantium and then Constantinople grew and prospered, walls were erected cutting off more and more of the peninsula, but always stretching from the Golden Horn to the Sea of Marmara. These walls had lasted an amazing 1000 years and were breached only in a mighty battle in the fifteenth century.

Much later the grand city known for so long as Constantinople, city of Sultans, with its tall minarets, church spires and elegant mosques, would finally be called Istanbul.

I was enthralled by the romance of its story.

The Ottoman Empire, of which Constantinople, then Istanbul, became the capital, was to grow in size and power until it became one of the largest and longest-lasting empires in history. I was aghast that my schooling had completely omitted to mention such an important power.

The end of World War I heralded its demise, as it had joined the 'wrong side'. Its lands were divided and its power smashed by the victorious Allies.

The new Turkey was created from the ashes by a nationalist movement and the amazing contribution of one man, Mustafa Kemal, later called Ataturk, now revered throughout the country. We had seen many examples. In every village there were statues of Ataturk in the public squares, and his portrait dominated every office and public space. His image was as ubiquitous as Queen Elizabeth's in the Australia of my childhood.

Accidentally Istanbul

I read how his legacies were many in the Istanbul that became the centre of his power. His grand yacht still floated, like a precious treasure, on the Bosphorus. His palace had become a vast museum and his humble two-roomed private quarters had been kept just as he left them at his death in 1938. The new society was based on the French philosophical thought that he revered. It had been conceived among the fairy-tale minarets, domes and ruins of the past, but it was largely his own creation. He was a giant: Ataturk, Father of the Turks.

With wildly conflicting feelings, reluctance mixed with trepidation, I read on, preparing myself to discover modern Istanbul from our grand black apartment.

4

Osman

During that fateful drive from the airport, affronted as the incessantly smiling driver invaded our space, I had gloomily surveyed the blocked six-lane motorway, the thick, fetid air, the grey sky and the dilapidated, dirty buildings. Every side street had seemed rubbish-filled and crowded with people.

My spirits had lifted a little as we drove along an esplanade with the sea stretching on our right. 'Marmara!' the driver had announced. We had reached the splendid waterway where the Golden Horn meets the Bosphorus: suddenly, as through a doorway.

The vast waterway, blustery in the salt-misted afternoon wind, was busy with fishing boats, ferries and parading ships. 'Wow!' It was awe-inspiring. Great clouds of seagulls were racing and hovering, and across the white foamy sea was a hazy distant

Accidentally Istanbul

shore. As we rounded a bend, between the crumbling city walls and the sea, the European slopes of Galata came into view, Galata Tower standing solid and imposing above a slate-roofed vista of tightly-crammed buildings. Of course, I didn't know then that it was called Galata Tower, but it dominated the shore like a stocky sentry, guarding the pink and grey and ochre buildings below it. On our left were the towers and turrets of the grand Topkapı Sorayı (Topkapi Palace) and in the distance a skyline of domes and minarets.

In that moment I recognised images from my childhood storybooks: fairy turrets where princesses lived and princes climbed to rescue them or kiss them awake. Why, *this* is where these towers were, those princesses. This was the faraway land of the stories.

'*Evet, cok guzel*' (Yes, very beautiful). Our driver brought me back to the present with yet another delighted smile.

I had wanted him to slow down, but we were carried on in the surge of traffic. I twisted round myself to look back. The grand view was lost but now I saw palaces, fountains and mosques slotted in among tawdry modern office buildings. Then we moved through a sea of apartment buildings and substantial private houses. We stopped in front of a grey and featureless block of flats surrounded by bushy gardens and a dusty parking lot. Was this where we were to live? My apprehension returned and my back started to ache.

Once the cleaners had left that first day, we found the kitchen to be a bare shell, without saucepan or cup. The stove was gas-

Accidentally Istanbul

fired but there was no PortaGas cylinder. Weeks ago in a telephone call, a University administrator had said: 'Bring nothing—just your clothes. We will provide everything!'

In the main bedroom we had found only a brand new doona and some sheets on the queen bed, virginally wrapped in plastic. At least we had bedclothes—but no towels, no soap. I had flopped down in one of the black leather chairs feeling that all my forebodings were coming true.

'This is ridiculous. What do we do now? And where are we? Where's the University from here?'

Ted pulled out his mobile and tried the cell phone of the President's secretary, but it was engaged. He sat down heavily opposite me. Just then my own mobile rang.

'Hello,' said a softly lilting Turkish voice. 'I'm Osman, friend of your friend Ruth in Australia. Do you remember? I played backgammon on the Internet with her.' His English was perfect, but with a detectable British accent laid over the Turkish.

'Of course, of course Osman—I remember you. Ruth emailed us about you.'

Ruth was my brother's friend and had once been a keen backgammon player, reaching out to others on the Internet. When my brother told her we were heading for Istanbul, she had told Osman.

'I've never met him, but he's also an architect. You may have something in common,' she had said.

On the phone, Osman said: 'I think you've arrived in

Accidentally Istanbul

Istanbul—yes? Welcome. I hope that you're comfortable.'

I giggled at this timing and tried to hide any alarmed edge to my voice. 'Well, Osman, I'm sure we shall be—but at the moment we're a little puzzled …' Then I blurted out our predicament.

Osman's gentle voice changed to one of authority. 'I'll be there in a few minutes. What is the address?' he demanded.

'We don't know. The driver said Attila. Do you know Attila?'

'Attila?' He had obviously never heard of it.

A different approach was needed. 'Our flat is on the third floor and directly over the road we can see a sports stadium called the Boğaziçi Üniversitesi Spor Merkezi.' Pronunciation being beyond me, I spelled out the words, describing 'g with a little scallop on top' and 'c with a cedilla'.

'Ah, yes, yes, yes—in Attila,' he said with a laugh in his voice. 'I think I know where that is.'

Ten minutes later Osman Taneri, handsome and stylishly dressed, with the soft brown eyes I came to expect in Turkish men, was in our new living room. He barely took the time to greet us before he was on the phone to the University. One didn't need to understand Turkish to understand the sternness of his tirade.

'It's appalling,' he then fumed, pacing the black carpet. 'Just appalling.'

I was fascinated by his telephone tone. 'Do you know them at the University?'

'No'. He was vehement. 'I don't need to know them. They

Accidentally Istanbul

cannot treat our guests from another country like this. I said I would speak to the President.'

Did he mean the President of the university or of Turkey? I was a long way from understanding the subtle gradations of class and education at the root of Istanbul society.

After he and Ted had exchanged pleasantries about architecture, he explained that the new campus of Bahçeşehir University was not far away, on the edge of the Bosphorus. Then he disappeared back to his appointments, leaving us to wonder at how quickly he had rallied to our aid in the middle of a working day.

'I liked him,' said Ted.

'It's amazing how kind he was,' I agreed. 'He has never met Ruth. All he did was to play backgammon with her for a few months.'

'We're going to have a good time here,' said Ted. 'I just know we are! Come on—it's time for dinner. There must be restaurants somewhere. Get your skates on.'

So we went walking to find something—anything—to eat. Sure enough, around the corner we could see shops in the distance. As we approached, the footpath which had been pleasantly tiled, narrowed and became rough. It seemed that every shop had created its own section: at different levels, of different materials, sometimes with cramped home-built steps down to a cellar in the middle of the footpath. *How ridiculously dangerous,* I thought. *The local council must get sued all the time*

Accidentally Istanbul

when people fall. How naïve I was then …

The street was busy with chattering young people who were instead walking on the narrow road, competing with the busy car traffic, slowing it to walking pace. There were cats everywhere, some streaking off, others watching warily. They were well fed, but some were dirty. *Maybe sick, or old,* I thought. Their food was scattered on messy newspaper sheets and there were some small cardboard cat boxes. My stomach recoiled. *Why don't these people feed their cats inside?*

We came to a row of small shop-front restaurants, each one crowded with more young people in jeans and T-shirts, satchels and papers spread around. I guessed that they must be students. The menu was in Turkish so we ordered what we knew: *köfte* (Turkish meatballs) and *künefe* (honey-tasting dessert made of crunchy fine 'straw').

'Do you have wine?' Ted asked, and added the Turkish word: '*Şarap?*'

The waiter lifted his chin, but made no reply.

'*Şarap?*' Ted repeated.

The waiter lifted his chin again, pointing out of the restaurant. I understood immediately. It was BYO. But the building he was pointing to looked like a mosque. In spite of this, Ted was already half-rising from his seat.

I sighed. 'You can't buy wine at a mosque.'

But then there was a subdued laugh from the next table, and we realised that some students had been listening in. *How rude,*

Accidentally Istanbul

I thought.

A doe-eyed boy leaned across to us, while his friends watched. 'He means that they are not allowed to serve *rakı* since they are so close to the mosque. That's the law. I think you need to be more than 500 metres away.'

Forgetting the wine, Ted was soon chatting animatedly with the students. They told him about their own university, just a few steps away from where we were eating. We called the waiter again and asked for water by pointing to the students' glasses. This request was much more successful. We were to learn that raising one's chin—or even more subtly, raising one's eyebrows—is the universal body language in Turkey for *no*.

The food was delicious and amazingly inexpensive. The cooks, lined up in their open kitchen just metres away, beamed at our obvious enjoyment.

With nothing in the house to eat—or eat from—we were back the next morning for breakfast.

'*Kahvalte?*' enquired our host.

'Breakfast,' said Ted, with smiling determination.

He was nodding rapidly. '*Kahvalte,*' he repeated. In a very short time he was back and, with a flourish, produced two large plates. On each was a warm pastry that wafted mouth-watering cheesy smells through the restaurant. Beside the pastry were olives, odd-looking cheeses, quarters of tomato, a hard-boiled egg, a small school of anchovies and some slices of what looked like French baguettes.

Accidentally Istanbul

'I was going to order bacon and eggs,' Ted grumbled, grinning. Unable to communicate, we ate what we had been given.

'I'm leaving the olives,' I said. 'I am simply not eating olives for breakfast. That is *quite* ridiculous.'

Osman's indignant telephone call worked—or maybe what followed had always been planned. Before the morning was out there was a knock at the door and I found a line of delivery men shouldering boxes of all shapes and sizes. In and out the men went, for half an hour. The boxes contained everything from kitchen equipment to a 12-piece dining set, and included a washing machine and a vacuum cleaner.

By the time they were finished, we knew that we had indeed needed to 'bring nothing'. But I was still slightly annoyed, as well as puzzled. *For weeks they knew we were coming. Why didn't they arrange for all these things to be delivered just one day earlier?* But I pushed my irritation aside as practicality took over. Since we were to be here for some months, it was no use fuming.

5

Getting to know you

Osman began phoning every day to enquire how we were, as though he had adopted some stray mentally-backward children. And we needed him. The simplest tasks became problematic. Without Turkish, I could not even make a phone call to find out what we needed to know—or even how to have one connected. Osman seemed to think of every potential problem before we did, facilitating our dealings with university administrators, electricians, gas suppliers, telephone companies and cable TV organisations. He told us where to post a letter and buy bread. 'Ask Osman,' we laughed as a mantra to each other when we found a new comprehension challenge. But there was part of me that wasn't amused. Everything was hard—harder than I had thought. In all my previous extensive travelling, there had been a hotel with an English-speaking receptionist to smooth

Accidentally Istanbul

away any difficulties.

Not only was Osman kind, he was charismatic as well. Fortunately his English was very colloquial, which made communication easy. We met his English wife, Diane, and I warmed to her immediately. She had lived in Turkey for 35 years and was still a great beauty, with fresh English skin, blue eyes and a torrent of blonde hair. Through an Internet game of backgammon, a real friendship began.

We did try to become as independent as possible. One morning I was composing an email to update family and friends.

'What's our address?' I asked Ted.

'I've no idea. It's not on any of the University papers. I know—I'll go and look at the street names below.'

He was back in ten minutes, triumphant. 'I've got it,' he announced. 'The building is called *Osman Konak*, the street is *Nispetiye Caddesi* and we're on *Itiniz 3*.'

'What's *Itiniz*?'

'It's the floor we're on. I worked it out from inside the lift. It says *Itiniz 1*, *Itiniz 2* and *Itiniz 3* at our floor.'

I sent this address off to all our friends:

Itiniz 3, Osman Konak
Nispetiye Caddesi Road,
Etiler, Istanbul

Letters and parcels then reached us without delay, and it was not until months later that I learned in a department store that the word for a level or floor of a building is *Kat*.

Accidentally Istanbul

'Then what does *Itiniz* mean?' I asked the shop attendant who had told me to go to the 4th *Kat,* then considerately translated this as 4th Floor.

'*Itiniz?*' she said, surprised but kindly. 'That means *Push.* Why do you ask?' I started giggling helplessly.

I couldn't stop laughing. For several months, we'd circulated our address as 'Push 3' instead of 'Level 3'. As I walked away her eyes followed me curiously, no doubt wondering what on earth she had said that was so funny.

Not long after we had arrived, there had been a knock at the door and my thoughts had turned immediately to proselytising Mormons. Instead I found an ample young woman with a mass of dark curly hair, alabaster skin and black-brown eyes, expensively dressed and wearing pearl stud earrings and a broad smile. In a flurry of Turkish she held out a plate of little chocolate cakes.

'I'm sorry,' I said immediately, endeavouring to be polite. 'I don't speak Turkish.'

She went on talking.

'No—no cakes today, thank you.' I shook my head as pleasantly as I could, and stood back with my hand on the door, signalling that the conversation was over.

She frowned prettily, eyes crinkling, and held up her hand to stop the door closing. She pointed to herself, then at the door of the only other apartment on the floor.

'Oh!' I breathed, embarrassed. 'Hello! You live over there. I understand. I'm so sorry. Please come in.'

Accidentally Istanbul

I took a step back and waved her in, but she smiled and persisted in Turkish, pointing to herself and saying what sounded like *Gyool, Gyool.* Then she pointed at me questioningly. 'Nancy, Nancy,' I said, nodding back.

She pushed the plate of cakes into my hand and retreated to her apartment, waving airily, smiling almost mischievously over her shoulder as she disappeared. I was left standing alone at my open front door holding the plate of cakes.

And so was born an unlikely friendship. *Gül*, Rose in English, was back knocking the next morning, with a man whom she introduced as *kapıcı*, or doorman. Sevget was a broad-faced, round-shouldered man of about 50, with a shock of thick, slightly-greying hair. I was to learn later that a *kapıcı* fills a general caretaker role and lives on the premises.

He shifted uneasily from foot to foot. They both came into my hall, but wouldn't venture further, no matter how much I suggested coffee. Without a word of English, they explained with many gesticulations to the space between our apartments, that if I could get a basket (Gül showing hers hanging on her front door) the *kapıcı* would bring fresh bread (*ekmek*) every morning, and a newspaper (*gazette*). I was to pay once a week. Then they rubbed their fingers together in the ubiquitous symbol for money (*para*).

I fetched my wallet. As I opened it, Gül took it from me as easily as if it had been a biscuit or a book. I was so shocked I didn't resist. The two of them pored over it with great

Accidentally Istanbul

equanimity, riffling through the banknotes and extracting what I needed to pay in a matter-of-fact fashion. Then they handed the wallet back and nodded happily, as though what they had done was the most normal thing in the world.

I told Ted what had happened over dinner that evening.

'So what did you arrange?' he asked.

'I know some kind of bread and a newspaper are going to arrive every morning.'

'Then we'd better go and find a bloody basket.'

We had found that shops typically stayed open well into the evening, so we scoured the nearby ones and found a proper hanging basket. Sure enough, from then on the English-language newspaper, *The Turkish Daily News*, and a loaf of very light white bread was to be found in our basket seven days a week, delivered by the *kapıcı* himself. Every morning my heart was warmed by the sight of the English news and the bread nestled together in the wicker basket. It touched me, this seven-days-a-week routine, the very *foreign-ness* of it.

I couldn't help mulling over the way that Gül and the *kapıcı* had riffled through my wallet. In all the years that Ted and I had been married, and as much trust as there was between us, I had never once opened his wallet. It was a violation, terribly impolite—yet they had done so as innocently as children.

How much this small gesture meant to us! Reading that paper every morning was like opening a window into Turkish society and politics. A confirmed news-lover, Ted was ecstatic

Accidentally Istanbul

to discover access to a world of riveting intrigue, which I also found well worth entering.

Like peeling an onion, day after day, layer after layer of complexity revealed itself. We drank in the news like famished desert travellers, and it led to endless discussions.

There was a lot going on. Turkey was on the brink acceptance as a candidate for European Union membership. This was before the global financial crisis and seemed a particularly good idea; it would have made Ataturk happy. We read, in less-than-perfect English, that there were, however, significant barriers. Many in the other European countries were outraged at the idea. The European in the street imagined a flood of Muslim Turkish workers arriving in Europe, with unknown consequences. 'Guest workers', *gastarbeiter*, from Turkey, mostly from the very lowest level of society, had led to stereotyping. Ignorance and parochialism can always be counted on to cause divisions.

How much the recent terror attacks in the United States, London and Madrid had fuelled the fear of Turkey's membership was hard to tell. The new-found desire by European governments, as opposed to their people, to welcome Turkey into the EU, may have stemmed from the same attacks; it seemed that the United States and Britain, both openly keen for Turkey's membership, were searching for a viable link between the Christian West and the Muslim East. Turkey could, as one pundit conjectured, be a showcase for the compatibility of Islam, democracy and secularism.

Accidentally Istanbul

But there were other barriers. Firstly, Turkey's constitution allowed great power to the military, with the role of safety-net or protector. The notion was that they could rescue the country if secularism and democracy appeared under threat. The feelings of Kemalists—those who believe in the legacy of Ataturk—verged on reverence for the army.

Then there was Turkey's troubled human rights record. For a long time under the previous regime, the police had had a free hand to jail and torture at will. It would take time for this culture to be changed. But the government appeared determined to do so.

The Armenian massacres or genocide during World War I were also a significant stumbling block. Was the killing of a large number of Christian Armenians simply part of the tragedy of war or was it intentional genocide? They were referred to only obliquely in the Turkish press.

For some years all these factors had made Turkey's proposed membership verge on the Utopian, but the current government, swept to power in 2002, had been making diplomatic inroads, unaware of how soon Europe was to crash into economic disarray.

We were intrigued at the complexity of the forces at play. The life around us on the Istanbul streets seemed superficially light-hearted. The cafés and tiny streets were full of laughter. It was difficult to imagine that somewhere close by momentous events were unfolding.

Accidentally Istanbul

Turkish people we met with new-found friends, in the street or on buses, seemed endlessly enthusiastic about discussing their politics. Deeper conversations were confined to those who could converse in English. The reactions from the educated élite, universally of secularist mind, were against the new government, whom they suspected of being closet fundamentalists. Among these people was a great suspicion of the Prime Minister, Recep Tayyip Erdoğan, and his AK (Justice and Development) Party. They were religious conservatives, and their power base was the vast numbers who were religious and poorly educated, we were told. The favourite conspiracy theory was that Erdoğan was moving the country towards the European Union because, in order to join, Turkey would have to curb the power of the military. Since it was they who had traditionally protected the constitution against the erosion of secularism, the loss of its power would allow Erdoğan, at the last minute before acceptance, to change Turkey into a fundamentalist state.

This seemed far-fetched, since I read that Erdoğan himself had been a victim of political repression and jailed for five months by a previous government. But then I read that the cause of his imprisonment was a speech at an election rally: 'Minarets are our bayonets, domes are our helmets, mosques are our barracks, and believers are our soldiers.'

The Opposition, the Kemalists, seemed to have an only vaguely-defined position, which approximated 'whatever Ataturk would have wanted'. Their core values were nationalism and

Accidentally Istanbul

secularism, goals dear to Ataturk's heart. To an outsider this seemed to equate to 'modernity at any cost', even if that could plainly be seen to cut across the civil rights of individuals, as in the case of a headscarf ban. I couldn't help wondering if some of these people were just pathetic and mindless followers of the West.

We were enthralled but sceptical. We knew that there were changes occurring and that Erdoğan and his team were moving rapidly. We read how a girls' education program was to convince parents in the rural east to send their daughters to school instead of keeping them home to learn field-working skills. Such articles were a clear reminder that Istanbul is not Turkey, with a depth of difference between the sophisticated west and the rural east.

Australia is indeed the lucky country, I thought, with no sense of smugness. But there was a spirit here that was exciting and contagious. Alongside these great questions, the Australian political system suddenly seemed banal. I began to be infected by the sense of 'real' events happening in Turkey, a momentous forward movement. Yet I was an interloper, outside the window watching a party going on, but not part of it. I longed for something similarly inspiring in the land of my birth. Australia seemed to have no real issues to deal with, and few goals.

Our conversations, these lessons, these thoughts, this newfound fascination, did not happen all at once, but slowly, over several months.

After my friendly next-door neighbour's cakes had been eaten, I returned the plate shining clean. Later an English schoolteacher friend told me that was a gaffe. 'Nancy! You were supposed to return the plate with your own gift of food. Here you never return an empty plate.' Seeing my crestfallen face, she continued: 'Never mind—they know how ignorant Westerners are. I'm sure she won't hold it against you.'

I felt unreasonably abashed. Would Gül think I was ignorant or just rude? Both were equally undesirable. The phrase uttered by my new English friend echoed through my days: *They know how ignorant Westerners are ...*

6

İstiklal Caddesi

Ted blew in like an afternoon breeze after his first day at the University.

'How was it?'

His big expansive grin was all the reply I received. I loved that grin—but it could be frustrating. He headed for the bathroom. 'I'll tell you on the way. Quick: put your shoes on. There's a film festival with a documentary tonight on the life of the great American architect Louis Kahn. I studied Kahn at University. Irem has told me where to go. Get your bag.'

'Who's Irem?'

'I'll tell you on the way.'

I was hurried out the door, laughing at how impetuous he was. We caught a bus on the street right outside our building. Now it was time to hear about his day.

Accidentally Istanbul

From the classrooms on campus, Ted told me, there was a splendid view of surrounding gardens and the Bosphorus. The other lecturers spoke excellent English and were very welcoming.

His classes were to be in English, without translation, since fluency in English was expected of all university students. We had learned earlier that most tertiary education classes in Turkey are in our language, something introduced in 1923 by Ataturk, who rightly predicted that English would be the international language of the future. At the same time he changed the Turkish alphabet from Arabic to Roman characters, to make the transition easier.

Ted was to discover, however, that this rule was sometimes more honoured in the breach than the observance.

That evening we took our first bus ride in a very new, clean vehicle, with no graffiti. Holding my hand in the sticky warmth of the crowded bus, Ted explained what he had learned. 'Town', where we were going, was Taksim, the very heart of modern Istanbul. The Old City, Sultanahmet, on the far side of the waterway known as the Golden Horn, is a living museum of civilisations dating back over 2000 years and a Mecca for tourists, and is packed with touristy shops and bazaars. But Taksim, and the suburb of Beyoğlu that surrounds it, are where modern Turks gravitate to have fun or do business.

I had my own small news. During the day I had resorted to the Internet with the idea of finding a job teaching English. Applying turned out to be amazingly easy and I had sent off

Accidentally Istanbul

three CVs. Taking independent action had lifted my spirits.

'Who knows whether I'll get a reply?' I said, feigning light-heartedness. But the more I thought about it, the gloomier I felt. They probably had long queues of job-seekers.

Alighting from the bus in the vast, cobblestoned Taksim Square was a shock to every sense. We were plunged into the middle of thousands of rushing, chatting, shouting pedestrians and in a dazzle of brilliant lights from the surrounding buildings. Again I felt overwhelmed. Pedestrians charged or straggled in groups on to the wide roads around the square, daring to pick their way through heavy traffic. Zebra crossings were ignored by both cars and people.

The huge enveloping crowds made me clutch my shoulder bag tightly. *I hate these crowds,* I pouted to myself. *I just wanted to go sailing with Ted, in peace.*

But the crowds were unthreatening. People were laughing freely, sometimes in jocular groups, sometimes in pairs. They were mostly young and clad in tight T-shirts and jeans, the girls chic and casual with many midriffs showing, the fashion of the moment.

Following instructions from Ted's colleague, we headed for Istiklal Caddesi, Independence Road. If Taksim had been overwhelming, this was an eclipse. There was no time to think as we were swept along in a sea of shiny dark hair moving down the street before us. In 25 years of concentrated travelling to many countries, I had never seen a walking street so crazy with the noisy vitality of thousands of strolling people.

Above us towered suites of elegant Edwardian buildings, some four to six stories high. Inside every lit window people were eating and drinking. The air in the street was suffused with the smell of grilled chestnuts wafting from colourfully-painted barrows. Others sold sweet-corn and some kind of fresh bagel. A hubbub of hawkers sold socks and bird whistles, scarves and earrings. *Lara's Theme* from *Dr Zhivago* soared above the general clamour, played by a man with a whistle at his mouth. The achingly beautiful tones swooped and flowed around us, adding a surreal touch.

Ted was entranced. 'Look—look at the buildings,' the architect in him demanded. 'It's mostly nineteenth-century design—but there's so much else as well. Look—there's a Victorian-era building right next to a Baroque one. That one is Renaissance in style; this is Greek. How extraordinary! They're all jammed together like an architectural museum …'

'Right,' I echoed, uncomfortable and nervous, realising my passport was in my bag. *Stupid. I should have left it at home. How am I going to survive for five months in this place?*

An ancient but brightly-painted red tram was pushing its way through the crowds, its bell sounding. It was crammed with the dark silhouettes of passengers and trailed by a crowd of boys clinging to the back steps or mounted on the mud-guards.

'That's totally dangerous,' I said. 'Those kids aren't more than ten years old. Where are their parents? Why do the tramways

Accidentally Istanbul

allow that? Someone is going to get killed.'

Ted didn't even hear me. He was still absorbed in the buildings.

The crowds seemed to be walking in a chaos of different directions around us. 'Where are they all going?' I asked, incredulous. Off to either side we glimpsed alleyways where people sat on tiny chairs sipping tea. We passed fashion boutiques, galleries, coffee houses and tiny, gaudily-lit restaurants.

We found the movie house down a side street. The polished timber foyer was crammed with people talking in groups, waving across spaces, laughing. We were just in time for the start of the film but someone ahead of us turned and said in English, looking at me: 'There are no seats left.'

I took a deep breath. Ted had been so looking forward to this surprise pleasure. Now among the tightly-packed crowd there was mumbling and grumbling, with many disappointed faces, just like ours. Then, surprisingly, we heard a speech somewhere and the crowd started to surge forward, carrying us with them. The organisers, rather than disappoint us, would allow us into the theatre.

After a rush of gratitude I thought: *What about fire?*

Soon we were seated with all the others, sprawled in every aisle and corridor, or standing at the rear. Darkness descended and the audience became quieter—but only a little. In this moment between reality and life on the screen, we were swallowed by, and became part of, the soft chatter of the anonymous human

Accidentally Istanbul

shapes around us. Anything seemed possible. A curious calm descended around me like a mist. I sat low on the steps and felt comfortable for the first time in Istanbul, surrounded by the soft rumble of Turkish voices. I felt I was on the same wavelength as the swaying, whispering bodies around me, even though I still clutched Ted's hand in a tiny but tight embrace.

7

Work—and an accident

When the phone (thanks to Osman) rang the next morning, I was delighted to hear it was the Berlitz Language School. A delicately-accented voice asked me to come immediately for an interview.

'Do you know where Istiklal Caddesi is?' she asked.

I couldn't keep the laughter out of my voice. 'Istiklal Caddesi? Oh yes—of course.' It was the *only* street in the whole of Istanbul that I knew.

I came away with a job offer from a tall, languorous Englishman. After a week's training, I would become an English Instructor. I was inspired, as I made my way home, by the thought that I would no longer be a mere tourist. I could immerse myself in Istanbul: catch a bus, walk down the street to the school, meet colleagues each day. For the first time in the new city, I felt

Accidentally Istanbul

a rush of adrenaline, of enthusiasm and, more than anything, a desire to understand the people from whom I felt so different.

The Turkish Daily News hinted at deep divisions in the society. The Kurds, the world's largest ethnic group without an independent state, settled in Turkey, Syria, Iran and Iraq, had long wanted their own homeland. They had not been given it when borders were drawn by the Allies after World War II and the more radical had formed what was now labelled a terrorist organisation, the Parti Karkerani Kurdistan (PKK) or the Kurdistan Workers' Party. It was banned in Turkey, Europe and the United States. Turkey seemed to fear for its territorial integrity: that the Kurdish dream to form Kurdistan would eat into Turkey itself. The previous summer a team of Turkish special forces, on a mission against the PKK over the border in Iraq had been arrested, blindfolded and hooded by United States forces. This had shocked the Turkish public. If the United States could carry out sorties into Iraq, would Turkey be next?

Mulling over such thoughts I started my week's training, little knowing the comedy of disasters waiting just out of sight.

It was just four days later, before my training was finished, that Marie, another trainee, and I visited a nearby upstairs-downstairs café in a lunch break. After we had eaten, we descended the stairs to the cash register, where smiling faces were calling '*Teşekkur ederim, afiyet olsun*' (thank you, *bon appétit*) which, curiously, they seem to say *after* meals as well as before.

As I was about to give a cheery reply I had the sensation of

Accidentally Istanbul

starting to fly forward—*a step, did I miss a step?*—and felt the floor rushing at me as my hands went splaying. Marble floor, *thud*, cold marble, white nothing but whiteness ... time passing ... now lots of men's shoes beside me ... men standing over me. Waiters? I looked up to see that they were all staring in the same stunned fashion and Marie was bending over me from behind. Everything had an air of unreality.

But reality returned in a rush when I tried to stand up. I found that one of my feet inside my running shoe had radically increased in size and was ballooning out of the shoe. The pain was making me nauseous. Worse, I reflected, if my foot was broken it spelled the end of my teaching career before it had even begun.

This moment of private black humour was rudely checked by my next thought. *Where will I find a hospital? A doctor?* Swooping regret overwhelmed me. What were Ted and I doing here in this strange country? *Serves you right.* I could hear my mother's words crashing in from the past. *Serves me right for what?* I silently asked her. *For being in this country at all? Yes, maybe ...*

The pain turned into hysteria. I started giggling, still half-bent forward. 'I'm so sorry for all the trouble,' I said to everyone and no-one.

My immediate future was decided by the others crowding around. I could hear the word for hospital, *hastane*.

'No, no,' I insisted. 'Taxi is good. I'll be fine soon.'

I was half-led, half-carried to the door of the café. There followed a one-footed hopping walk, with waiters on each

Accidentally Istanbul

side helping, to where I could find a taxi. Two waiters and the manager had left their posts at the restaurant. *Who's looking after the customers? I should have paid for the coffee,* I fleetingly thought and even muttered. No-one answered.

Marie was walking with us. 'Don't worry about anything,' she said.

But between waves of pain I was still worrying about the customers abandoned back in the café. 'Go back,' I urged as we reached the line of taxis. 'Thank you, thank you. Marie, please tell Berlitz I'm so sorry I can't finish the course.'

I flopped into the taxi, glad for a moment that I didn't have to move or be polite. *Home, for ice. Better than a hospital. There I might have to wait for hours*—thinking of Australia. I really had no idea about the waiting time at Istanbul hospitals. *Then maybe later hospital for treatment ...*

I phoned Ted. Thank God he was at home and able to meet me at the front door.

Stupid step, I fumed, *stupid, stupid, stupid.* The marble step I had missed was indistinguishable in colour from the rest of the floor. *This wouldn't have happened if we hadn't come to Istanbul. Stupid Turks—why don't they make their buildings properly? Why didn't they mark that step so you can see it? Wouldn't happen in Australia; we wouldn't allow it.*

My gloomiest thought was that I wouldn't be able to teach. *What shall I do? Stew in that black apartment by myself all winter? How I hate this place!*

Accidentally Istanbul

That night I dreamed of wild sailing, squalls riding over the sky dumping heavy rain and driving the boat over the waves, with me at the bow. But if I was on watch I should be behind the wheel, while Ted slept. In the dream the sea was alive with dolphins that turned as they leapt, then gazed at me for a crazy moment before splashing back into the sea. They were accusing me of something. Abandoning the wheel? I tried, but my foot wouldn't budge and I couldn't get back to the cockpit.

I woke tangled into the sheets, wondering where I was. Then I came down with a thud to reality. The lights of Istanbul cast a glow through the window. I sank back into a light waking sleep accompanied by a strange, unhinged feeling I couldn't shift.

8

Life on crutches

I was given crutches at the pristine, efficient and very high-tech Amerikan Hastanesi (American Hospital). I don't know what I had expected, or why I thought that it would be dirty or ineffectual. It was in fact far more modern than hospitals I had experienced in Sydney. We were whipped through to see a doctor seconds after a patiently impatient Ted and I arrived.

But doesn't Australia have the best medical system in the world? I felt a sudden surge of private embarrassment at my assumption of superiority.

'Istiklal Caddesi is a walking street. How did you get from the restaurant to the taxi?' Ted asked that evening over dinner, after he had grilled a steak for us.

'It was a bit of a blur, but the waiters, two of them, and the manager almost carried me down to the road.'

Accidentally Istanbul

I paused, sipping my wine, thinking.

'I think there were only two waiters in that café—and both walked out and left all the other customers.'

'Mmmmm,' said the ever-articulate Ted, slicing into his rather strange Turkish cut of steak, which he had served with a salad accompaniment.

This was such a surprising country. Waiters would certainly not leave their posts in such a way in Australia.

One of the disadvantages of being afflicted in a foreign city is the lack of family and friends. Gül was kind, but without a shared language, our communication was friendly but superficial. My loneliness added misery to the pain, and for the next few days I was swept into a dark place, imagining all the support I would have received at home. But even while I languished in self-pity I couldn't help laughing at my own dejection. I followed the news on CNN, read *The Turkish Daily News*, wrote emails home, and watched the worst possible American movies—anything to pass the time.

Outside the sun glittered and tittered at me, a callous autumn light. The Call to Prayer five times a day penetrated my skull. It sounded like someone being tortured. Below me on the street I could see people fortunate enough to be able to walk. They floated past easily on both legs in gloriously-coloured summer clothes, laughing, turning, bumping into one another and sharing jokes to which I was not a party.

My misery deepened.

Accidentally Istanbul

Even when I could bear to put a foot to the ground and started using crutches, I tended to crawl around the flat because it was more comfortable than hobbling. Ted thought this was hilarious. 'What about crawling out and getting a cup of tea, Nance? No, no—I'm joking. I'll get it.'

After a few days, when I could put my foot to the floor without breaking out in a sweat, I phoned the Berlitz Language School, full of recovered bravado.

'But we were told that you have a broken foot and that you're on crutches.'

'Yes', I replied sweetly, moving into my prepared speech, 'but there's nothing wrong with my mouth.'

So I started as a hopalong teacher, catching taxis, which effectively cancelled out my income. I tried to keep a smile on my face, but large dark spirits came welling up out of a black gulf, overwhelming my attempts to be positive. *What am I doing here? If I hadn't come to Istanbul my foot wouldn't be broken.*

As the days passed and I could move outside, however, I was at first puzzled, then intrigued, then mollified by people's reaction to my bound foot. Queues of able-bodied taxi-hailing Turkish people gave way to me, gesticulating that I should take the first taxi. Did they think I would use my crutch as a weapon?

'No, it's fine—you were here first,' I would protest. But I was always overruled with much waving of arms and indecipherable Turkish words delivered at bullet-fast speed. They would take my crutches and shoulder bag and shove me into the taxi, returning

Accidentally Istanbul

them when I was safely seated. I would make ineffectual grabs at the bag (*the effrontery of it!*) but would get the first taxi, even from a long queue, every time.

Soon, becoming braver and feeling more sure of my ability to negotiate the world with one foot, I returned to travelling by bus. This was even more astonishing. The buses in Istanbul, a city of over 20 million people, are invariably crowded and bus-stops bulge with waiting commuters who press forward as a vehicle approaches.

Except when I was there.

As I became used to my new treatment, I began to feel like a queen as they made a path for me. If anyone who hadn't noticed was still pushing, a quick jab in the ribs would make them turn, startled, then shrink back, allowing me a pathway as befitted my station as newly disabled.

On the crowded buses several people would at once get up. I *always* had a seat. Then there were the bus drivers. Often a grin and a wink would usher me into the bus without payment. I also learned, as I hobbled to a bus stop, to examine the ground. If I so much as glanced up, a bus driver would squeal to a stop to offer me a ride.

My thoughts flashed randomly, unbidden. *Is it because I'm a foreigner? Do they think I may be contagious? Or are they simply kind?*

Crutches were also great conversation-starters, and, surprisingly, many fellow passengers spoke English. It was here

Accidentally Istanbul

on the bus that I learned that useful phrase *Geçmiş olsun,* which doesn't exist in English. Its literal translation is: 'May it pass quickly' and it is used for any misfortune.

'*Geçmiş olsun.* What did you do to your foot?' I often heard beside me in soft, halting English, which led to many conversations. I returned home not only with stories about my new students, but also with tales of the interesting people I had met in transit.

'He told me he's studying law at Bogazici University. He's the first one in his family at university. Next year he's applying to Harvard.'

'She used to live in Ankara, but now lives here, near her grandchildren. She was an English teacher at a private Istanbul school, and had me laughing at her stories of the spoiled children of the rich.'

I learned interesting facts about the demographics of Turkey. Istanbul has a very, very rich élite, about 5 per cent of the Turkish population, who enjoy wealth beyond the imaginings of Australians. While we would have half-a-dozen billionaires, Turkey has at least 40. The next category would roughly tally with the *lifestyle and expectations of Americans*, in the words of my bus sociologist. This category, I learned, took in about 15 per cent of the population. The other 80 per cent were *dirt poor*. I didn't yet know how to check these facts—which, once we learned more, turned out to be surprisingly accurate.

Ted benefited from his spouse's temporary disability. Many

Accidentally Istanbul

restaurants refused to accept a tip, gesturing at my crutches as though that should have been explanation enough.

Life began to find a rhythm, the rhythm of city life anywhere in the world: the rush to work, the rush home, the traffic, the rush in lunch-hour restaurants. But there were differences that, in spite of my reluctance, I couldn't help noticing.

Soon I realised that my experience as a disabled person wasn't so different from what others perceived as needing help experienced. All over the city I noticed young people helping the old or disabled: giving up a seat, helping them across a street, standing back to allow them easy passage. Sometimes these helpers were shop assistants, sent out quickly by the shop-owner to assist.

I was amazed one day to see both the conductor and driver abandon our bus in the middle of a busy traffic lane to assist a large elderly woman slowly and painfully alight. Then, together, they carried all her shopping to the footpath. While I stared, no other passenger seemed to notice. Cars following didn't blow their horns. Our world froze for a few moments while these kindnesses happened in an invisible bubble.

One night in a busy restaurant, an old drunk, a rarity in Turkey, wandered in, staggering against one of the tables. Two waiters immediately dropped everything and went to him, soothing him for a while, talking softly. Then a kitchen-hand appeared with a plastic box of food and the waiters disappeared into the night with the old drunk, abandoning the other diners.

Accidentally Istanbul

I asked the people at the next table: 'Where are they taking him?'

In excellent English, one explained: 'Oh, they know where he sometimes sleeps at night. Maybe he's hiding from his family. It's sad that the restaurant doesn't know where they are, but they take him back to the park with his dinner.'

We were all left alone for about 20 minutes, no orders taken, no meals served. The diners went on chatting as though nothing unusual had happened.

Such incidents softened my heart towards Istanbul and its people. Maybe I was going to enjoy our winter here after all.

At night, however, I dreamed more and more about sailing. Sometimes the stars came down to the boat and surrounded me in a blazing aura. Sometimes they fled and the sky was dark with squalls and heavy rain. The nights I dreamed of moonlight were the best, with the air thick with flying-fish and the sea sparkling. Strangely I always ended up somewhere on the boat I shouldn't be, out of control, flying up the mast or trailing behind it in the air. Always I felt at fault, guilty that I was not steering. In the end these dreams always woke me, fear and guilt driving me awake.

9

A Turkish friendship

As time went on, almost every day Gül knocked on my door with gifts: vegetables, luscious tomatoes, celery, carrots, biscuits, eggs and more home-made cakes. Why was she so, so generous? It was beyond anything 'neighbourly'. I had known good neighbours in my small-town childhood, but this was Istanbul, a city of 20 million people and growing.

Now that Osman had stopped phoning so often to see what further catastrophe had befallen us, if a problem arose I called on Gül. This typically happened when a strange man appeared at my door with official-looking documents accompanied by an explosion of fast Turkish. When I looked blank they would repeat what they had said louder and faster. I learned to cry *Anlamadım, bir dakika lutfen!* (I don't understand. Please wait a minute!) and cross the hallway to knock loudly on Gül's door.

Accidentally Istanbul

She was always the soul of helpfulness. I would stand by like a five-year-old, listening, while she ignored me and solved the problem without further reference to me. And there were many bureaucratic problems in Turkish daily life. If I had to pay money, I paid. If I had to sign my name, I signed. If it had something to do with the flat rental, she would phone the University and solve it with them.

All the while her food presents kept coming. My measly attempts to reciprocate were met with horror. *Hayir, hayir!* (No, no!) she would say. In any case, because I knew little about many of the ingredients in the local shops, I was flat out making dinner, let alone thinking what to give her as a treat.

Gül was always dressed carefully, with jewellery, often pearls, and her curly hair left loose and bouncy. She explained as best she could with great sweeps of her voluptuous arms, that she had home-grown the vegetables and raised the chooks herself, somewhere far, far away.

I loved her visits, even though I was continually mystified at why she would offer such unconditional friendship. Did she pity me, alone in a strange country? Was it merely because I was a foreigner and she thought she should be hospitable? Or was this the way of all Turkish neighbours? I had no way of knowing. She entered our flat floating in a cloud of goodwill, exuding enthusiasm, constantly ready for a laugh, grabbing my hand to sit me down to explain something.

As my Turkish improved, our friendship deepened and

expanded. It took a long time for me to accept that it was simply friendship she was offering and that there was no hidden agenda.

She seemed certain that I would reciprocate, and I didn't want to disappoint her. I took this more and more seriously as time passed and I came to know her family as well.

Her husband Şeref was an accountant in private practice. As solemn as Gül was sparkling, he remained aloof from the fun that she generated, as if tolerating an irritating child. He was punctilious in dress and never without a tie, even at weekends. Their two sons, Ali, 19, and Fehmi, 17, were both students. Ali was to go into his father's business. When I innocently suggested that he must like accountancy, he paused, his face falling from cheerful to wistful.

With a small frowning smile he explained in his uncertain English: 'I must.'

These two words, delivered quietly, with settled resignation, appalled me. He had communicated an ocean of feeling. Not allowing himself to dream, he was corralling and confining his energies, his thoughts, his potential, to the service of what he saw as family duty.

Later I would find this attitude common. Grown-up children were bound by the invisible glue of family obligations, caught in a web of love that was stronger than any dream of an alternative world, stronger than the lure of any unexplored talent. But it was this first encounter that dismayed me.

When Ramazan (Ramadan) arrived, their household, like

others, rose in the dark, so that Şeref could finish breakfast before daylight broke and the time of fasting began. Gül explained matter-of-factly that she and the boys had a blood condition that allowed them to avoid this obligation. I listened, nodding, but heard no echo from within. The Muslim faith was too far removed from me for a useful reply. However, the sceptic in me wondered if such a 'condition' allowed a respectable escape from an arduous religious duty.

I was both too reticent and too lacking in Turkish to embark on such a delicate enquiry.

10

The fruit of the land

'I don't need my crutches any more,' I told the world in general. I was balancing my crutch-less way down the hallway, one tentative step at a time.

'You look to me as though you still need them.'

Ted was leaning against the end wall, silhouetted against the light behind him.

'What do you mean! Look—I'm hardly limping.'

He grinned. 'Sure. But by that scrunched-up expression, I'd say you're trying to break your foot again.'

'Don't be so gloomy.'

Once I was able to throw away the crutches, life expanded into a routine: teaching, exploring Istanbul in our spare time—and cooking meals. These presented me with a real dilemma.

'Cooking is impossible in this country,' I grizzled to Ted one evening. He, to whom the concept of cooking belonged on another planet, merely said: 'Mmmmm.'

'I went to that supermarket round the corner today.'

'Right.'

'They've got nothing.'

Now I had his interest. 'What do you mean? They had a whole market full of stuff when we went there together.'

'Yes, but we were only looking for the basics: tea and flour and coffee and salt. When I looked closer today they have no bacon, soy sauce, wasabi, no proper cheese, no oyster sauce, fish sauce or ginger—and all the herbs have Turkish labels.'

'Well, that seems reasonable. We are in Turkey, Nance. What about a dictionary?'

'I tried that, smartypants, and our big English-Turkish dictionary has *no* herbs listed.'

'I'll write them a letter. You didn't really expect to find bacon in a Muslim country, did you?'

'Since this is supposed to be a modern city, I thought maybe …' I trailed off, irritated, by Ted, by the non-European language everyone spoke, by the lack of bacon. *If we were in any European country, the herb name would be almost the same.*

Ted was smiling now. '… and after all, wasabi is Japanese.' I ignored that.

'And the meat is ridiculous—it doesn't even *look* like beef or lamb,' I continued. 'The only thing that looks familiar is chicken.'

'Right. So what are we having for dinner?'

Accidentally Istanbul

'Chicken.'

A few evenings later Ted cut into his meat, smelled the portion, then put his utensils down again.

'What's this?'

'I'm not sure. Maybe mutton.'

'It doesn't taste like mutton.'

'No—and it doesn't smell like it either. I just pointed it out in the window to the butcher. What do *you* think it is?'

This time he put the portion into his mouth and chewed carefully.

'I don't know. It's not chicken. Maybe it *is* mutton.'

He started eating and I did too.

'These are potatoes—but what's the green stuff?'

'I don't know that, either. I thought they were a sort of bean, but they fell apart instantly when I cooked them. Sorry if they're a bit mushy. I put lots of butter in them to make them taste better.'

'Remember that great little restaurant we went to on our first night here?'

'Yes.'

'Why don't I take you out to dinner?'

The solution, was, of course, obvious. I bought an English-language Turkish cookbook, deleted all the files in the recipe corner of my brain, and began cooking Turkish.

This made an adventure of every meal, since I tried a new recipe every day. Ted kept reassuring me that he didn't marry

Accidentally Istanbul

me for my cooking skills. Eventually I produced some delicious meals and we adjusted very nicely to eating— more or less—as our neighbours did.

I never had trouble with rats or cockroaches in my Istanbul kitchen. I remembered how difficult it always was to rid houses near the water in Sydney of rats and cockroaches. Even though the Turkish communal rubbish-collection system was less than perfect in some places, garbage left to lie in the open for long enough to become nose-rocking and eye-repelling, nowhere did I see vermin, even in the most remote and neglected back streets. This was a vast, ancient city, crumbling and full of alleyways and dark places. It was also a port, with ships arriving from far and wide. It wasn't until I reflected on the vast number of street cats everywhere in Istanbul's streets that I realised what was happening. After that when I saw food left in an alley for the street cats, I spared a thought for how they spared us from vermin.

Each Saturday we joined the trail of Turkish people dragging shopping trolleys to the once-a-week fresh produce market or bazaar, just a walk away from our flat.

The bazaar was held high above the Bosphorus under rows of tent-flies flapping in the wind. Local families mingled with students from the nearby university and came away dragging wheeled bags burdened with rich-smelling fruit and vegetables.

Under the tent-flies was a low and constant hubbub of incomprehensible conversation. Every stall offered slightly different produce. We found dark red tomatoes, bright yellow

Accidentally Istanbul

corn, lustrous black plums, long elegant leeks, and a hundred other types of fresh vegetables or fruits, some unknown and some quite strange: deep red carrots, odd-shaped beans, strangely-shaped seeds in hessian bags. Fresh artichokes were flat, but about the diameter of a cantaloupe, and floated in water. Men busily cut pumpkin into pieces. I laughed in sympathy. *Yes, pumpkins are really hard to cut, aren't they?* What I didn't yet know was that Turks serve pumpkin as a sweet, never a vegetable.

The strong aromas in this busy canvas world included the sweet smell of manure-filled soil and fresh-cut herbs. The produce had obviously come straight from the farms without ever seeing a refrigerator. Many pieces still had twigs attached or were bunched together on branches.

The eggs were sold in tens. *How strange*, I thought, brought up on dozens. They came precariously packaged in plastic bags, many covered in chicken fluff or smeared with traces of poop.

If we paused in front of a stall, the owner, with the twinkle of a smile, would often offer samples of his produce. What a surprise to the senses! Juice dripped from fruit and garlic alike when cut, and the herbs were rich in flavour.

Olive oil was sold in old Coca-Cola bottles. Even this was offered in tiny lids for us to taste. Some oils were rich and yellow; others were different shades of green. I was told how the oil, called *sızma,* meaning leaked, referred to the method of making it. The farmer puts the olives into a stone vat with a tiny hole towards the bottom on one side. He then places a

Accidentally Istanbul

matching stone on top, and as they are crushed by the weight of the stone the oil leaks out into the waiting Coke bottle. The resultant oil is pungent, with the smell and taste of fresh olives, different tastes from different types of olive tree.

Home-grown walnuts and almonds were sold by the bagful, cheap and tasty. One farmer made bread every week in fat cobs. These became a weekly necessity. The cheeses had a range of acrid tastes, light and vinegary. When one stallholder offered us some, he bleated like a sheep, causing his colleagues to chuckle. Getting into the spirit, offering another he made butting motions like a goat. We laughed and nodded, accepting hesitantly, but relishing the strange tastes.

One of our delights, after we began to be a regular sight at the bazaar, was getting to know the stallholders. Each called *Hoş geldiniz* (Welcome) as we approached.

Hassan explained in kindergarten English that he was actually a magician, but *now that times in Turkey are so bad*, was selling fruit and vegetables from the farm *until things improve*. He would always try his latest magic trick on us, pulling tomatoes from his ear or eggs from his sleeve.

Nilan was a spice merchant. The stunning scents and aromas from her stall spread over all those nearby. She sold 100 different freshly-ground varieties.

After passing through the fruits and vegetables, other stalls sold an amazing array of goods, from safety pins to home-made soap, wooden spoons, local jewellery and towelling, dried fruit

Accidentally Istanbul

and nuts, biscuits and hammers and laundry baskets.

Ahmet was a wood-worker and sat surrounded by his wares, from breadboards to walking sticks. Ted had dreams of starting a walking stick collection, so he had one made to order. With no language shared, I watched a comedy of hand gestures and smiles while Ted tried to make what he wanted clear. Ahmet would take no money in advance and seemed quite offended at Ted's offer.

A week later, the walking stick did not disappoint. It was the product of beautiful workmanship, finely carved. Ahmet glowed with pride as he presented it to Ted with a slight bow.

When samples were offered, rejection would always offend. As I began to understand a little Turkish and the young studs who ran the stalls became used to seeing us, I began to glean that they were calling me, not the distant *Madam* that one might expect in the West (or worse, *Luv*), but *Abla* (Older Sister), affectionate yet respectful, inclusive and warm. I felt a curious rush of warmth towards these simple folk. Honoured. How strange to feel a connection with such people. I had no sense of my own smugness, or of the contradictions in my response.

While we most often went to the bazaar which was closest to us, there was another which was so unusual it seemed one of a kind. Up by the Black Sea, some 500 kilometres from Istanbul, is the heavily-forested province of Kastamonu. At midnight every Saturday night the farmers of Kastamonu rise from their beds, get into their trucks loaded with the freshest of farm

Accidentally Istanbul

produce, and drive through the night to the city, arriving in the salt-misty airs around 6am. They park in a back laneway in the Kasımpaşa suburb. There, in the next couple of hours before the Istanbulites begin to stir, they erect their tents.

As we would arrive, canvas canopies would be flying high like white angels, keeping off both sun and rain. Housewives, many dressed in simple muted floral headscarfs with conservative coats over their ample figures, scurried and bargained. The noise was deafening, with the Kastamonu merchants shouting each other down. This place was known simply as the Kastamonu Bazaar, and we heard that some of Istanbul's top chefs frequented it to find the best produce.

What a feast for the senses it was! All the common vegetables and fruits were there—but there was so much more. I read, once I knew of its existence, that there were over 800 foods that were exclusive to Kastamonu. Walking the alleyway where the farmers noisily displayed their wares, I could well believe it. There was home-made bread of various sizes and shapes; fresh rose-hip and celeriac; radishes the size of large tomatoes; and fungi of a dozen varieties, the most interesting being orange with green mould edges. There were vegetables so strange that I could not get their names translated. There were many smooth jams in great barrels made by the good citizens to be ladled out by the gram, and great canvas bags of nuts, all hand-picked from their own trees. There were sweets made from tomatoes, egg-plant and walnuts.

Freshness was the key. In the poultry section, hens, ducks and geese were all still alive. The stallholder would slaughter them after you had made your purchase. I did not stay to watch.

Both Ted and I were entranced by these bazaar experiences. What was it that made us love them so? I started to think it was something deeper than merely the smells and tastes of fresher food. The experience left me with more questions. Was it the increasingly plasticised versions of foods eaten in the West, obtainable year-round because they are kept in cool-rooms and doled out on demand? Was mine a search for a new way of eating? Had I been missing the feel of the earth at some deeper level? We Westerners seem alienated from the planet that gave birth to us in a way that is quite disturbing.

Finally it was the tomatoes which were the most surprising and memorable. Dark and richly red right through to the core, their perfume was heady and their taste thrilling. I resolved never again to shop for supermarket tomatoes.

'They must have such rich soil in their farmlands,' observed Ted as we wandered one day.

'Yes, very good soil,' said a young, accented male voice. Surprised, we swung round to see. A young man sat behind a table of vegetables, cleanly dressed and with smart slicked hair, smiling in amusement at Ted's comment.

I smiled back, keen to speak with someone who spoke English. 'This is your stall?'

'This …' He paused, hands on hips, swaying from foot to foot, '… is my family's stall. We have our own farm just 20 kilometres

Accidentally Istanbul

from Kastamonu.' There was warmth and pride in his words.

We looked at his array of shining fruit and vegetables, cleverly arranged into perfect mounds. When I looked up he was watching me, with a slight, almost affectionate, smile.

Though the crowds were dense, for the moment there were no customers.

'So how many of these vegetables do you grow?' I asked.

He looked slightly injured. 'All of them. Everything here is direct from our farm, except for the pumpkin, which is grown by our neighbour. She's too old to sell her own now.'

His English was, so far, very grammatical.

'And does all your family speak such good English?'

'No—I'm the only one. None of my family speaks English at all. I am very good at it, and I'm only helping my father out during my holidays to give him a rest. In September I'm going to attend Boğazici University.' It was the university near where we lived.

'Congratulations,' I said, intrigued. 'You must be looking forward to it. What are you studying?'

'Engineering. Yes, I'm the first in my family who goes to university.'

Eyes shining with an almost electric pride, he looked nothing like my image of a university student. Hair immaculate, clothes neat, he stood tall as a good soldier. He would certainly be an oddball at an Australian university, with the students' accent on grunge. Even the notion that he was looking after his father's

Accidentally Istanbul

business *to give him a rest* instead of insisting on his holiday rights before going back to school interested me. I amused myself wondering what my kids would have thought when they were teenagers had I told them they were to look after my business during their school or university break while I 'rested'.

We chatted for a while about his father's farm and his young sisters, who were very bright at school and hoped to go to university too. As we wandered away, his image stayed with me, unusual, stimulating, inspiring even. He was obviously proud of his father's stall, and of his family. If I had known then that Boğazici University was one of the most difficult in Turkey to get into, I would have been even more impressed. But as with many things, I didn't know. I didn't know.

11

Teaching in Istanbul

My first day at the Berlitz Language School, on the sixth floor of an ancient building in Istiklal Caddesi, had arrived. I had studied the syllabus they gave me and it didn't seem hard, but I had not taught school of any sort since I was 18 when, as a new graduate from Queensland's University of Technology Teachers' Training College I taught for four short months before fleeing into a career in television.

Now here I was resuming teaching decades later, mere bravado having carried me this far. In front of me, ranged around a large table were a dozen faces, dark-haired, pale-skinned, brown-eyed. *They are beautiful people,* I thought. Sleek cheek-bones, aquiline noses, sometimes the hint of Asia in the elongated eyes. Now all these eyes were directed seriously at me, expectantly, raising my adrenaline. Could I deliver?

Accidentally Istanbul

'Hello!' I began brightly ...

The students ranged from coquettish young women to middle-aged businessmen but they behaved in that first lesson like frightened children. They wrote down everything I said in their notebooks and sat neatly in their places, hands folded, not speaking unless directly asked.

That evening I was dejected. 'They act as if they're *dead*,' I wailed to Ted over dinner. 'I can't work it out. Surely I'm not so scary?'

'You're scary to me sometimes,' he said, attacking his steak.

'There's some kind of barrier between us I can't pull down,' I said, ignoring this. 'They're too disciplined. It's as though they're automatically scared of teachers. Maybe they're just wary.'

I went to bed but didn't sleep for many hours, dispirited by my failure to enliven the students. Had I made some fundamental mistake, thinking I could waltz into another country where I knew nothing of Islamic culture and make a success of something I had only practised long ago?

I was awake before the Call to Prayer wavered into our bedroom. Doves were cooing somewhere outside the window, raising my spirits, but cheerlessness followed me out into the day. Again in my classes the students were attentive but distant.

A new friend and confidant who had lived in Turkey for many years explained that old-fashioned teaching methods dictated that students had to offer extreme respect to all teachers. Strict discipline made them passive and docile. Teaches disseminated and students accepted, with no question or analysis. So different from our system

The breakthrough, when it happened, came suddenly a couple of days later. I was testing them on the vocabulary given for homework and pointed to a picture of a cup.

'What is that?' I asked.

First student responded: 'That—is—a—cup.'

Me: 'Very good, yes. Now—' to the next student, pointing to a fork, 'what is that?'

Second student stood up, took a deep breath, then shut her mouth rapidly and paused, before slumping back down into her seat. Obviously life had been too distracting in the past few days for her to commit the word 'fork' in English to her memory. Her pantomime of trying to give an answer and failing made me laugh.

Without thinking, I then folded my arms and shook my head slowly in mock-disgust. The result must have been comical, because the class giggled uncertainly, exchanging glances. This surprised me. Encouraged, I held up one hand, palm down, and smacked it with the other, still shaking my head disapprovingly, but with a small grin.

This time there were guffaws. Some of the girls opened their mouths in shock and covered them with their hands, still giggling.

Even the girl who hadn't done her homework laughed. Obviously, trying to be comical was not normal behaviour for a teacher.

Accidentally Istanbul

It was like a door opening. Soon, with the use of wry comedy, my class began to unwind and relax, displaying a love of humour. Finally they became as rowdy and engaged as any Australian group of uninhibited teenagers, while remaining respectful. I was *always* addressed as Miss Nancy, for instance.

Although they were aged between 20 and 40, they crowded around me between classes like a gaggle of kindergarteners, each wanting to talk individually. One afternoon, a young woman called Emine stayed behind seeking help with some homework she didn't understand. Just as we were about to leave, she stunned me by saying conspiratorially: 'You know, Miss Nancy, there is something I must tell you. I am Kurdish.' I didn't know what to say. She seemed to be taking me into her confidence. Was she testing me? Was this identity something hidden from her colleagues? Was prejudice so prevalent? I smiled and responded with something innocuous. So much to learn ...

Irritated by the students' tendency to lapse into Turkish when stuck, the next thing I instituted was a 'fine cup'. Anyone who spoke Turkish during the class would be fined the sum of 50,000 *lira* (about five cents), to be put towards a party at the end of term. This simple act had the effect of galvanising the class into uproarious self-discipline, so much so that the neighbouring class teacher knocked on our door to ask if we could be a little quieter.

After answering the door and receiving this haughty message, I tiptoed back to my desk, forefinger to lips, begging my class to be quiet. There were explosions of almost-silent laughter.

Accidentally Istanbul

At the end-of-term our rambunctious class passed their exams with flying colours, the most successful of all the beginners' classes. I was so happy I floated through my days as though I had won a million-dollar lottery.

Ted's semester was passing quickly. Though I wasn't sure how soon after classes ended in mid-January he would be free, I was sure that by February we would be sailing again.

My other class was very different from the beginners' one. I travelled by taxi twice a week to the Nike company headquarters. My group of four were each around 30 years of age, upwardly-mobile executives. However, these four young men were obviously not from privileged backgrounds. Since English is a prerequisite for all those who wish to work or study outside Turkey, élite families make sure that their children grow up bilingual.

These promising executives were being schooled for better things within the international Nike company. On my first day they couldn't hide their astonishment when I hobbled into the boardroom on crutches.

I used my old line: 'Don't worry—my mouth works well enough.'

They stared blankly at me. 'Oh, er sorry—I meant that even if my foot doesn't work very well I'm still able to *talk* to teach you.' By then this didn't sound funny even to me.

They continued to stare blankly.

A new approach was clearly needed. 'That was an English joke. Maybe I can explain it later. My name is Nancy. Why am

Accidentally Istanbul

I on crutches? A couple of weeks ago I broke my foot, but I only have to stay on crutches for about six weeks. It won't affect our sessions together.'

I then asked if they had any questions about the course before we began.

One young man sneaked his hand up. 'Do we call you Miss Nancy or Teacher?'

'Just Nancy will be fine, please.'

Another hand went up. 'Please, Miss Nancy, I didn't understand what you said about your mouth. Did you hurt your mouth too?'

'No—but we can talk about that during the lesson. Any more questions?'

Thus encouraged, the first young man put his hand up again. 'Miss Nancy, I am sorry to ask this question, but I am confused. We were told that we were to have an Australian teacher. But you speak English *very* well and you tell us English jokes, not Australian. I think you are English, not Australian, yes?'

On this note we finally began the lesson. I found their English language fluent but not grammatical, so there was much that I could easily contribute.

Back in Istiklal Caddesi, being involved in the administration of the Berlitz Language School was also a steep learning curve, but one that had little to do with education. Almost without exception, the visiting teachers, in Istanbul on a contract that included accommodation, were dissatisfied with their living

Accidentally Istanbul

standards, usually a room in a shared flat. The complaints were endless: 'My room is too small ... the plumbing doesn't work properly ... my flat-mate smokes too much ... he doesn't clean up enough ... cleans up too much so I can't find anything ... stays out too late ... goes to bed too early so we can't make a noise ...' Their expectations of the standard of the flat they were allocated usually far exceeded what was provided and many of them returned home within weeks.

As for the administration of the School, it seemed to take three times as many people to carry out a task as I would expect. Office workers—and there were so *many* of them—stayed at work a long time, well into the evening when they could have been better employed enjoying Istanbul's lively nightlife. They wandered around ineffectively, chatting to one another, seeking lost files, staring into space. I was nonplussed but fascinated.

In the evenings, Ted and I entertained each other with tales from our teaching days.

'I reckon they think of me as some kind of comic relief,' he said one evening.

'Who? The students or the teachers?'

'The lecturers. The students are no problem. They all understand English pretty well.'

'But don't the lecturers speak English too?'

'Yes of course—but not to each other in the staff office.'

Of course, I realised. *Why would you speak a foreign language to compatriots?*

Accidentally Istanbul

'So you don't know what the Hell is going on?'
'Not a clue. Everyone shepherds me around making sure I know where to go for any meeting. "Come on, Mr Ted," they say. "This way, this way—we have a staff meeting now."'
We laughed together.
'But they think I'm pretty smart.'
'What makes you think that?'
'Amazingly, I'm almost the only one on the staff who has any practical experience—and none of them has experience in multi-storied buildings. So I'm able to pick holes in student drawings very quickly. Some of the staff have even asked if they can attend some of my lectures on certain subjects.'
So far our Istanbul life was going well, much better than I had expected. But a small voice at my shoulder kept muttering: *This can't continue. Things are going too smoothly.* I was so right.

12

Claudia's foodie walk

As we roamed around the city I started to feel its magic in spite of myself. We became used to the high sorrowful keening of the Call to Prayer. At first I found it jarring and intrusive and made remarks about strangling and how much pain they must be suffering. But gradually I found myself waiting for the five calls to mark the progress of the day. As it vibrated across the valleys, I came feel warm shivers up my spine, thrilling to the exotic sound. The long, tremulous cadences echoed in my head and added a comforting feeling of normality: all's well. Unlike in Muslim countries like Oman, the Maldives or Yemen, we rarely saw people milling around outside the mosques. No-one paused or seemed to heed the sounds, just raised their voices a little louder in the cafes in order to be heard.

After a while I realised that all the people we had met since

Accidentally Istanbul

arriving, with the exception of Osman's wife Diane, were Turkish. Even though I loved these growing friendships, I found I was longing to speak English freely, without simplifying it and removing idioms. So through a contact I joined an English-language book club, and found a wonderful group of women with whom I could freely communicate. They were mostly permanent residents of Istanbul, many of them married to Turkish men, so their existence was grounded in our daily reality.

I learned so much from these women. The books they read, mainly focused on the Middle East, were exciting and stimulating and their political discussions erudite and original. I felt like an innocent sponge after a lifetime of drought.

Then there was Claudia. I didn't notice her at first, except on the far side of a room at functions. She seemed always to be the centre of a group, a vivacious woman with humour in her eyes, a smile always at the ready and a mass of dark, bouncy hair. I came to admire her forthrightness and bubbly way of lighting up every room she entered.

But it wasn't until we were talking of Turkish cuisine that I realised she was a woman who could unswervingly guide me into a greater understanding of Turkish culture. British-born, she had lived in Turkey for 35 years with her Turkish husband and knew its blemishes as well as its inspiring beauty.

It didn't take much discussion to find that Claudia was a keen foodie who loved to cook and discover new tastes, smells and experiences.

Accidentally Istanbul

'The cuisine here is so fascinating,' she enthused one day in her softly-cushioned home, surrounded by treasures gathered from around the world. 'You and Ted should come with me on a foodie walk.'

'What on earth is that?' I laughed. 'Of course—we'd love to.'

One chilly day we arranged to meet in the lively heart of modern Istanbul, at Tünel, the entrance to one of the oldest underground railways in the world. The story went that during Ottoman days, French traders whose ships were moored along the coastline near the Golden Horn liked to live at the top of the nearby hill to catch the cooling breezes. So they built the underground railway in order that French ladies and gentlemen would not break into an unseemly sweat by slogging up the steep hill.

To reach Tünel, however, we had to move through Istiklal Caddesi. It was always difficult to ignore the ever-present temptation to go wandering down every by-way and alcove of the fascinating walking street. On each side the elegant four and five storey terraces, once homes, were now shops, restaurants, galleries or coffee houses. Istanbulites young and old spent many hours in conversation here or playing backgammon in the alleyways, with tea in tiny glasses at a million *lira* (a dollar).

Then there were the nightclubs, antique shops and art galleries in the maze of small streets behind. Even more interesting were the artists' shops and studios, where the artist was often to be seen busy at work.

On the day of our walk, seagulls flew screeching overhead

Accidentally Istanbul

among the telephone wires as we wrapped our coats firmly against the autumn air and strode out. Meetings in Turkey are very warm. Everyone kisses excitedly on both cheeks, including the men. It had not taken us long to become adept. These are fleeting kisses, sometimes just a touching of heads. Though we were only three, it still seemed like a celebration, as though we had met in a desert after months of trekking.

We set off together down a crowded narrow street. Soon I noticed that most of the shops contained musical instruments: Western-style, such as violins, cellos and guitars, but also others, strangely-shaped and stringed. I lingered over long-necked lutes, tiny instruments smaller than a violin and large bulky objects.

'They're *saz* or *bağlama,* pronounced *barlama,*' Claudia explained, pointing to a long-necked instrument like a lute. 'They've been played since Graeco-Roman times. And this is a *tar,* which originated here and is thought to be related to the Western guitar.' We saw many lanky long-haired young men with large satchels slung over their shoulders, walking with a purpose.

'This is obviously a very strong music centre,' I prompted. Claudia smiled and nodded. 'They're very cool. I'm sure they're all determined to be famous one day.'

The way became steeper and steeper and seemed to be heading straight into the Bosphorus, far below us. Footpath stalls were selling fresh pomegranate and orange juice for a dollar.

'You *must* try one,' pressed Claudia, laughing at my screwed-up face. 'I can't believe you've been here so long without trying

Accidentally Istanbul

pomegranate juice–maybe with orange?'

But I tried it straight. The juice, called *nar*, was (for me) undrinkable: sharp and sweet, sending my jaw into a frenzy and my eyes into a waterfall. Claudia and Ted sipped theirs with expressions of rapture.

'Have you tasted *salep*?' Claudia asked.

'No—and I'm not going to if it's anything like pomegranate juice,' I said quickly.

Claudia, completely undaunted, strode off again. '*Salep* is the warming Turkish drink for winter: orchid milk. It's made from the root. It not only tastes delicious, but is also very good for curing coughs and colds.'

I could not imagine an orchid root as food, let alone a drink. We had reached the wide, flat cobblestoned square dominated by the vast old Galata Tower, with indoor/outdoor restaurants around it. Claudia led us into one of these and a rush of warm air pressed against our cold cheeks as we doffed our coats and rubbed our hands to get our circulation back.

While we sat and waited at a plain polished timber table, Claudia explained. '*Salep* comes from the root of one particular orchid. It has not one bulb, but two. One it uses for the coming spring, to make sure the plant survives. Our *salep*-makers only take the spare bulb, and the orchid then starts to make another for the following year—so Turkey's orchids will never become extinct. The bulb is then dried and crushed into flour, and from this the drink is made.'

Accidentally Istanbul

The *salep* arrived in three mugs, steaming, sweetly-perfumed and sprinkled with cinnamon. I could not tell if it was health-giving, but it certainly made for a welcome warming interlude in our walk.

While we sipped, Claudia told us how she had come to marry and live in Turkey. With three children now grown, she seemed buoyantly contented with her life with her Turkish husband, whom she referred to endearingly as T.

'You must remember that even though my diplomat father is English and my mother French, I never lived in England until I was sent there to complete my schooling, from the age of 11. Before that we'd spent time in the West Indies and then Swaziland. When my father was posted to Ankara, I was actually living in South Africa. Like the dutiful daughter I was, and not enjoying Africa much, I came to visit them for a while. I was just 22.

'I'll never forget my first sight of the Bosphorus. I arrived at Sirkeci Railway Station after travelling for three days from Venice on the old Orient Express. I remember coming out and seeing the Golden Horn and the Bosphorus and thinking "Wow!" I was smitten, totally and utterly smitten. All the people, the seagulls, the boats and the colour—even though it was December.

'Then I took the overnight train from Istanbul to Ankara. It was very like you imagine the Orient Express, with blue velvet seats and waiters and low lights.

Accidentally Istanbul

'When my family met me, they told me that Christmas was coming and that there were all sorts of functions on. I met a lot of people, and among them was T.

'I thought he was extremely good-looking, but I also met other young Turkish men who could speak English better than T—so all in all, I had a very good Christmas. Afterwards I decided to stay on here for a while.'

I was fascinated by Claudia's story.

'What did your parents think of T, and of your marrying a Turkish man?'

'They never said anything. I knew they liked him. The following year I returned to England to get a teaching qualification. While I was in Oxford studying, T used to visit my mother and bring her flowers. He was sweet—always very polite and correct. Yes, they liked him.

'It's been a wonderful relationship. T was everything I loved in a man, and my parents approved, as I did, of his family. I liked them all. It actually never occurred to me that there was anything strange about marrying a Turkish man. After all, I had already spent my life moving from country to country. It was another adventure.'

My second *salep* disappeared as fast as the first. Then we stepped out into the cold sunshine and plunged further down the cobbled hill, hands deep in our pockets for warmth. Finally we reached the coast and the Galata Bridge, where hundreds of Turkish fishermen, their dark jackets and trousers flapping in

Accidentally Istanbul

the breeze, were lined up catching their daily swag of small fish. Behind them stood an echoing line of black buckets along with all the fishing paraphernalia. Above the fishermen hundreds of seagulls floated and dived in the wind, and beyond and above, a little misty from the saltiness of the air, were the swooping lines of the old city. Further out was the Bosphorus, lined with great ships plying their trade between the Black Sea and the Mediterranean.

It was a scene that never failed to impress me. I stood, staring and breathing it into my lungs, like a drug.

I could hear Claudia's voice in the background. 'This way, this way. Come on—we're going to eat *hamsi*.'

She led us away from the bridge down some rough stone stairs and across a plaza where old men and young were selling fishing rods and mussels, freshly-squeezed orange juice and pen-knives, shoe-polish and tissues.

Ahead were fishing boats just in from the sea, and to the left a tent city of fish-sellers calling their wares. Hoses ran from the water over our walkway to the tents, and the fishmongers were constantly re-watering their fish, with many others in large vats, swimming in circles.

We watched, intrigued. It's hard to imagine fresher fish, and the milling crowds, with never a foreigner or tourist in sight, were testament to the popularity of these markets.

We moved a little further on to what was little more than a tent jammed between the fishmongers. Their calls were deafening, and with the additional row of the crowds and the motors of the fishing boats alongside, Claudia could only beckon. At the front of an open-sided tent was a rudimentary kitchen with large pans resembling woks, containing oil. Three men with implements in hand pushed fish around them. The tables in this tiny restaurant (for it *was* a restaurant) were minute, cocktail-table height, and the chairs little more than children's stools. We squeezed on to them, our knees pointing absurdly to our chins. The aroma of fish was fresh and alluring.

I looked around. The restaurant was full of dark-clothed men eating in a hurry.

'It's said they serve the best fish in all of Istanbul,' said Claudia, grinning mischievously at the apparent absurdity of her statement. The canvas flapped over us, caught on one side with plastic where it had torn. The kitchen looked as though it could do with a good scrub and the floor was the bitumen of the road. The little tables were stained wood with a knife and fork wrapped in a paper serviette slammed on the table in front of us by a waiter in black trousers and a crumpled short-sleeved white shirt.

'Right,' I said dubiously.

There was a short exchange in Turkish between Claudia and the young waiter and he hurried away.

'There are other things you can order—but *hamsi* is the speciality.'

Sure enough, almost everyone in the tent was eating a high mound of crisp small fish that appeared to have been fried in

Accidentally Istanbul

a little flour. Watching, I realised that the diners were chewing up the bones as well. There was a salad of rocket and onion on each plate and some lemon, but nothing else.

I can't tell you if this is the best fish in Istanbul—but it was quite superb. The sweet tiny fish we had been served had bones that we crunched as well.

In the months to come, we would return often to this tent. The bill seemed absurd: five dollars each for a full-sized meal.

'Yes, there was a lot—but that was just an entrée,' said Claudia, as she dragged us away from the tent-restaurant. 'Now we have to walk uphill again, so you'll be hungry by the time we get to the top. I have something really special for you there.'

We went through an inconspicuous door to find the underground railway station, the high walls lusciously decorated with richly-coloured Turkish tiles in traditional designs. We sped uphill in a black tunnel and arrived 45 seconds later at the top station of Tünel, where we had started.

'Now for the next course,' Claudia called back as she raced ahead. We followed her through the throngs down a sloping street to another square. A big man with a very large moustache and a smile to match, his vast stomach covered by a generous apron, was working at a hotplate fired with charcoal.

Claudia had a rapid conversation with him. 'This is the best cockroach of all the cockroach in Istanbul. And this is Nazmi Bey (Mr Nazmi), who has sold his cockroach right here for over 30 years, rain hail or shine, six days a week and has put his

Accidentally Istanbul

daughters through university on the proceeds.'

Nazmi Bey continued to smile merrily, nodding at her enthusiasm, even though he could not understand a word. I stared at the hotplate, transfixed, trying to form words. But when Ted spoke he was laughing.

'Now Claudia, much as we love you, I am *not* eating cockroach.'

She looked puzzled, but before she had time to answer, I intervened, knowing that the genial man in front of us could not understand.

'Claudia, you're not serious. Turkish people surely don't eat cockroach.'

She threw back her head in her hearty way, laughing. 'Not *cockroach*, silly: *kokoreç*. You didn't hear me properly. It's the lining of the intestines of the sheep. You'll see: it's delicious!'

After contemplating eating cockroaches, intestines didn't sound so bad.

'He's been here for 30 years—that's amazing,' I said tactfully. I don't think I quite believed it—even though I do now. We smiled our own greetings and relaxed.

Nazmi Bey began the complex task of creating 'the best *kokoreç* in all of Istanbul'. On the impossibly small area of his barrow he had minute horizontal skewers on which some kind of meat was revolving. As we watched, Claudia explained.

'Nazmi Bey is famous, because instead of using normal lamb he uses the sweetest of suckling lambs and then cooks them to perfection.'

Accidentally Istanbul

'So this meat is lamb?' Ted looked doubtful.

'No—lamb intestines. See how the intestines are stacked together round the skewer.'

With flourishes more suited to a temperamental orchestral conductor, Nazmi Bey chopped the intestines finely, slapped them between two halves of a loaf of bread and garnished them with rich red tomatoes and green salad. He then offered us either a quarter or half of the fresh loaf as though he were presenting us with a delicate rose.

'It's best that we share, because the most interesting course of all is still to come,' said Claudia. 'I don't want you to miss out by eating too much here.'

We were silent for a while enjoying the delicate flavour of this very unusual hotdog.

'I've already eaten too much,' I announced when I'd finished. 'What *is* the next course?'

But she wouldn't tell.

We headed further up the hill, passing specialist food shops. One sold only olives, another simply herbs and a third only tea. There were cheese shops, fresh chicken shops, pickle shops, all alluring, mouth-watering.

We also passed many inviting restaurants before arriving at our destination. It was not a restaurant, but another barrow jammed against the side of a building, with a few sparse chairs and tables spread around against the wall of a narrow alley.

I stared, somewhat bemused. 'Here?'

Accidentally Istanbul

'Sheep's head,' said Claudia.

'Sheep's head,' Ted repeated, to make sure he had heard correctly this time.

'Sheep's head,' I chimed in, half-waiting for her to correct us. Surely we couldn't be asked to eat the head of a sheep?

'Sheep's head,' said Claudia firmly.

'Seriously?' I said.

'Seriously.'

Suddenly a small man was beside her, beaming.

'*Merhaba, Muammer Bey* (Hello, Mr Muammer),' she exclaimed enthusiastically.

There was much smiling and Turkish too fast for me to follow. Muammer Bey, a small clean-shaven man with a wide smile, waved us generously towards small wood and iron tables. But first Claudia wanted us to see the raw sheep's heads. With the owner watching, she pointed out the cadaverous skinned heads in a glass window to the side of the barrow.

I could feel my stomach turn with nausea, but it was too late. Ted and I sat as we were told and waited, our coats wrapped tightly to keep out the cold wind, while Muammer Bey set about slicing our sheep's head. I couldn't bear to look.

As we waited, Claudia told me that he also owned the building next door, occupied by a restaurant. Many years ago he had become so successful that he bought the small adjoining restaurant building. However, he had acquired more headaches having to employ staff. His clients preferred the original little

Accidentally Istanbul

platform-in-the-alley and he wanted his simpler life back, so he returned to the barrow.

This tale will stay in my mind forever, as a warning that the outward appearance of success often does not tally with inward harmony. Wisdom is to know when you're happy and that it doesn't always equate with riches or the perceptions of others—a difficult lesson to learn.

The sheep's head was served sliced with onion and parsley with a sprinkling of thyme and red pepper. The meat was quite delicious: moist, tasty and cooked to perfection. We learned that it was actually a combination of the cheek and tongue of the sheep.

'No brains?' I asked.

'No brains,' was translated back.

We had enjoyed a wonderful morning with warm-hearted Claudia. As she departed she said: 'Now I must teach you some of my favourite recipes.'

'Absolutely,' I agreed. But that was for another day.

• • •

If you want to know more about Claudia's recipes or just love reading about tantalising food, go to her mouth-watering blog, http://seasonalcookinturkey.blogspot.com.au

13

The Bosphorus

We finally settled in enough to start to see the sights, meaning the conventional ones: the Blue Mosque, Aya Sophia, The Grand Bazaar, the old Roman Cistern and, of course, the mighty Bosphorus, dividing Europe from Asia and the only access to the Mediterranean from Black Sea ports.

Our very first voyage up the Bosphorus to the Black Sea seemed a simple adventure, with nothing to fear. We were to take the large government ferry: stable, comfortable, inexpensive and fast enough to do the return journey in a day.

'Come with me,' said a fellow teacher and friend, Filiz, a Turkish Australian lawyer here to 'discover her roots'. 'There's no commentary, so I'll come with you and point out the sights.'

I was delighted to have her company since she had excellent knowledge of all things Turkish. She began as soon as we left

Accidentally Istanbul

the wharf. 'Did you ever hear the story of the Princess who was kept in a tower and grew her hair long so that her lover could use it to climb up to her?'

Of course I remembered. I had mooned over the illustrations of the maiden whose hair fell hundreds of metres from her tall head-dress to the grass of the tiny island where she was captive in her tower. It was as much part of my tropical childhood as a snow-filled Christmas, in temperatures that sometimes reached 40 degrees on Christmas Day.

There were different versions of the story. One said she was so beautiful that her captivity was to deter possible lovers. Another told of her father hearing from a soothsayer that his daughter would be killed by a snake, so he locked her in the tower in a desperate attempt to avoid the curse.

Now, swishing through the waters as the engines purred, I stared fascinated at the Maiden's Tower, a small stand of rock in the middle of the Bosphorus, stark white in the morning sun. A shining haze of salt mist surrounded it, with seagulls and cormorants vying for space on the rocks below. The surf swirled and lunged roughly against the rocks. Truly, it would have to be a valiant lover to brave swimming the Bosphorus to reach his princess.

As a dreamer of a child, such stories had seemed more real than the small life of my Mum and Grandma and Grandad, and infinitely more alluring. At night my father would read me stories of a world which was somehow more perfect than

Accidentally Istanbul

ours, where life was always, after an adventure, lived happily ever after.

There was something unnerving about my dreams being exposed to the hard reality, as we drew closer, of white paint flaking and dripping with traces of rust, with flotsam of oil scum and plastic bottles mixed up in the foaming salt water.

We bought Turkish tea from the onboard cafe and sipped daintily (there is no other way to sip from a Turkish tea glass) as the sturdy old ferry, followed by flocks of greedy seagulls diving for thrown tidbits, thundered up the middle of the wide waterway.

The Bosphorus is full of currents and always dense with a plethora of vessels: small fishing boats, pleasure craft, the odd sailing boat, other ferries criss-crossing paths and great ships passing in a steady parade, one after the other. Along the foreshore vast old palaces, elegant villas, traditional Turkish wooden buildings and modern mansions climbed the cliffs.

Filiz kept up a constant account of what we passed. She showed us the last home of Ataturk in the Dolmabahçe Palace, and the forts, which also resembled those in my childhood stories, keeping the Turks safe from attack or invasion. But it was when we finally saw the Black Sea in the distance that Filiz softly offered her most explosive information.

'You know, it was here that the calamity happened that was the cause of Noah's Flood.'

'Noah's Flood?' I echoed. 'You mean the *Biblical* Flood?'

Accidentally Istanbul

'Yes of course. It was the flooding Bosphorus finally breaking its banks and gushing for the first time into the Black Sea that's said to have caused the Flood.'

I thought this was preposterous. Why, it was a Biblical myth, not part of history.

'But that was—,' I began weakly.

'Yes, a very long time ago: 5600 BC if two very smart American scientists are correct. Bill Ryan and Walter Pitman are their names. I've just been reading about it. They've gathered a vast amount of evidence to show that water levels in the Black Sea—at that time a big freshwater lake—had fallen a huge 120 metres below the level of the world's oceans, because during a very long cold period the snows to the north didn't melt, so the northern rivers stopped flowing into the lake.

'As the earth warmed, the oceans rose again and finally broke through the weakest part of the wall between the Bosphorus and the lake, creating today's Black Sea and flooding vast areas of what had been land.'

'If that's the case,' Ted interjected, 'that's why the Flood was able to be forecast, giving Noah some warning.'

I glanced at Ted to see whether he was serious. He was. In spite of my incredulity, as we approached the Black Sea, I could imagine the build-up of waters, and how they rose unstoppably until the vast Flood. 120 metres!

For some reason this amazing revelation, if true, was uncomfortable to me. *How dare the Turks take a Biblical story*

Accidentally Istanbul

and claim it for themselves? Though I had long discarded the notion that the stories of the Bible were factually true, they were nevertheless part of my childhood, belonging to all, not to be so simply owned, as it were, by one country or another. It was akin to being told that Uluru was actually the mountain that came to Muhammad.

'No, surely this can't be true,' the child in me protested. 'It's just some smart Americans trying to make a name for themselves.'

But maybe …

At the last port on the route, Anadolu Kavagı, we climbed a steep hill to splendid heights and the ruined Byzantine Yoros Castle. This was Genoese for many years until the Ottomans drove the Italians out after the conquest of Istanbul.

'They used to throw a chain across the Bosphorus from here to the other side to protect it from attack,' said Filiz, as we paused, puffing, staring out across the narrow waterway. *Fancy, a chain. Now we have satellites that will warn us.* The road to the castle passed handicraft stores, then old but shining-clean houses, with new paint glistening in the sun. Gardens were blooming and kids shouting and playing. After the grime of the city it was refreshing. Then the houses petered out, replaced by grasses and trees and the hill became steeper.

Finally, with relief, we were at the top. It felt like a precarious Top of the World. The misty Bosphorus stretched in one direction and the wide expanses of the Black Sea in the other, treacherous cliffs on all sides except for the steep road we had climbed. There was a wild wind up here too—small stabs of fear in the sunshine.

'See the rocks over there?' Filiz was pointing to a small cluster of black rocks on the far side of the Bosphorus, where it joined the Black Sea. 'They're the Wandering Rocks encountered by Ulysses.'

'You're joking,' I laughed. *Google will have the final say on this.*

Filiz's long dark hair glistened as she laughed back, smooth olive skin shining, startling blue eyes crinkled into the sun. 'I suppose you also won't believe that this is the path Jason took when he was searching for the Golden Fleece.'

'Filiz, I will believe that one of my favourite fairy stories, the princess in the tower whose lover had to climb her hair to reach her, took place in the Bosphorus. And I will perhaps believe that Noah's Flood was the Bosphorus breaking into the Black Sea. But this is going too far. You mean Jason of Jason and the Argonauts? Wasn't that Greece?"

'Of course not, silly,' retorted Filiz without hesitation. 'You have to rid yourself of thinking that everything worthwhile in history originated in Europe. Turkey seems to have been erased from our history books in Australia. All my Turkish history knowledge came first from my family.'

I looked towards Ted for help, but he was gazing up at the ruined cylindrical wall of the old castle.

'It's amazing,' he said.

Accidentally Istanbul

'Which—Jason or Ulysses?'

He didn't even look at me. 'The construction, the Byzantine layers. See the alternating layers of brick and stone ...'

'It's true,' I said to Filiz. 'My memory is that we knew Turkey only as Asia Minor.'

As a child, I had joined that great Australian institution, the Australian Broadcasting Commission's Argonauts' Club, in search for adventure through imaginary tales. My daily trudge to my Queensland school led through dry rocky pathways. I longed for adventure—perhaps to follow the lizards that slunk away under walls and rocks, to see where they went. Instead we kids headed for compulsory milk and the scratching of chalk on boards while we learned the Kings of England by rote. I *needed* the Argonauts.

For a time Ted, Filiz and I stood and stared, silent, in awe of both geography and history.

There was just time for a *Yarım ekmek balık* (half a breadloaf with fish) before the ferry left for home.

That night I dreamt of Mossman, my first home town. Grandma, ever-stern, hovered over the memory, which smelled of the soft gauze of mosquito nets over my messy sheets-kicked-over bed, my mother's kisses and the weekly chook running headless around the back yard followed by Grandad's laughter. The comfort of these images then disappeared as an earth-tremor shook the ground and we ran to the air-raid shelter. *Running. Running.* At the entrance to the shelter I halted, because there

Accidentally Istanbul

was a puddle of water too wide for me to jump. In the dream I couldn't get to my mother, who was already inside with dozens of others. Her hand reached out to me as she called. But I still couldn't jump the puddle.

In the morning I woke slowly: *sleeping awake, sleeping awake,* taking the dream with me, a feeling of flux, of not being grounded. It followed me into the day.

14

Refugees of Turkey

She had a thin face with shadows under her eyes. She was 11 years old, but tiny, so that she looked about eight. *Lack of nutrition?* She was warmly dressed, rugged-up against the cold in this twice-weekly class. There were coloured plastic clips in her hair, green and yellow and pink. Someone loved this child, cherished her, sent her out hopefully to school.

Now she struggled super-seriously with spelling 'do'. She wrote 'doo', then looked up, mutely pleading for help. I felt a familiar lurch in my chest but I grinned, shaking my head slightly.

Twice weekly was all the education children like her could get. They were from Africa, Iran, Iraq and their families were living illegally in Turkey. We were sitting in the nave of a church, given over for the school. *We don't proselytise* was a strictly-obeyed

Accidentally Istanbul

mantra. Above us archways swooped to the light, and the dark walls hosted plaques and carvings. They seemed to shrink away from the noise, music and laughter below. The altar, so used to genuflection, was ignored. Instead, we played and learned, then ate bread rolls and apple slices for 'breakfast'. The children drank bottled orange juice, while the teachers drank tea.

The little girl's name was Talya. She chatted on while furiously colouring in a picture. They had been in Turkey for eight years. Her mother wanted them to go to the United States, Canada or Australia, she said. The school headmaster had told me that such people were largely ignored by the Turkish government, which had enough problems of its own trying to elevate the standard of living of 70 million of their own citizens.

Who knew their background? We were not to ask. We simply taught, or tried to teach, the children. Their concentration spans were short. *Nutrition?* I wondered again. If something apart from the lesson attracted their attention, maybe a bird call outside or some laughter in the next class, they would simply run to it. They couldn't sit still for long, so this meant constantly changing focus.

There were just three children in my class. I could not have handled more. Their needs were great, their love of 'school' immense, and their knowledge of group behaviour non-existent. They all wore parkas because the chilly air in the nave froze our hands. Daniel, the boy in my class, wore a navy beanie and scarf wound around his head and neck, with only his eyes showing.

Accidentally Istanbul

He looked like a tiny cat burglar. He worked valiantly at his spelling.

Talya was still fascinated that I came from Australia. She chattered between laboriously drawing words in her school-provided exercise book. 'My mother loves Australia,' she told me. 'My mother says that in Australia there are sharks and kangaroos and koalas. My mother says we are going to Australia.' She paused. 'It's good in Australia. My mother says that you work for two weeks then have a holiday for two weeks.'

I smiled, aching with sadness, and didn't correct her. She rattled on obliviously, sitting in the coloured pools of light beaming down from the tall leadlight windows. Her world was her own, her dreams not to be destroyed. After applying for eight years, it sounded unlikely that she and her mother would ever set eyes on Australia.

My teaching in this church had evolved from a lunch meeting with a group of foreign friends, American, South African, Australian. In the conversation I had heard my name from the other side of the table.

'Nancy is a teacher.'

'Hello—who wants me?' I called, curious.

'A teacher at the refugee school has been transferred home. Don't you have a teaching qualification?'

How could I refuse?

I was still teaching English part-time at the Berlitz School, but this volunteer teaching of child refugees was where I felt

Accidentally Istanbul

most needed. Now I sat listening to my small students in this nineteenth-century Anglican Church situated in the old French Quarter. There were 23 churches in this area, all of them many hundreds of years old, a legacy of the tolerance of the Ottoman Empire, famed for allowing Jews and Christians to live in peace and prosperity—as long as they paid their taxes.

Political, diplomatic, and economic forces conspired against children like Talya. I learned that thousands of them were here with their families seeking asylum. The children were caught in a game they might never comprehend. Their families shared an illegal status that might or might not turn into designation as refugees. But finding a new country to accept them was never assured.

Talya's plight has to be seen in context of Turkey's own situation. As we read avidly, talked to educated Turkish people and to long-time foreign residents, a picture emerged. Because it was strategically vital to the international community, Turkey could see a bright future for itself: a surging economy, a rising standard of living and a progressive if conservative government. It acknowledged its problems: the wide gap between rich and poor, inept and corrupt bureaucratic structures, weak social welfare systems, and widespread difficulties for women.

The European Union was exerting complex and contradictory pressures on the country as prerequisites to EU entry. On the one hand, Europe was pressing Turkey to improve its human rights record and act humanely to asylum-seekers. On the

Accidentally Istanbul

other, it insisted that the government prevent the illegal flow of refugees into Europe.

To compound the problem, United Nations figures showed that the number of refugees accepted in EU countries had declined by almost 50 per cent over the previous five years. They had developed a 'fortress mentality'.

Meanwhile, even then, in 2006, thousands desperate enough came by leaky ship across the Mediterranean, or overland from Syria, Lebanon or other countries to the east—or they simply flew in and overstayed their three-month tourist visas. They came from all walks of life: doctors, bakers, shop-keepers, lawyers. Desperation was the common denominator.

No official tally existed, but governments estimated that there were between 500,000 to a million refugees at any one time in Turkey. I was aghast. I was moved to tears and anger about the numbers our politicians thought of as large for illegal immigrants in Australia. Here, some who had been refused refugee status took up lives in the chaos of winding slum streets in rundown buildings, firetraps, up to ten stories high with no lifts and little sanitation.

The children in the Christ Church refugee school were a mixture of those waiting for a status determination, those accepted as refugees, and those whose claim had been refused. Once I met them, they were not easy to forget.

On arrival, they would register with the United Nations High Commission for Refugees (UNHCR) as asylum-seekers, and

Accidentally Istanbul

the wait began. Most didn't know it, but the process might take four to five years.

Life was precarious. The families weren't eligible for health services, work permits or public education. Finally, even if they were given refugee status they had to wait for a country to accept them. This might never happen.

I became more and more curious about the children in my class. On enquiring, I found that if, at the first stage, refugee status was refused, Turkish authorities would give 15 days' notice to leave the country. Then, according to refugee workers, if the immigrants had money they could pay a smuggler thousands of dollars to enter Europe illegally. If not, they would typically go 'underground', disappearing from the radar screens of the authorities, officially ceasing to exist.

One day I was lucky enough to meet a worker from the Istanbul office of the International Organisation for Migration. 'With no ID they can't rent rooms legally,' he explained. 'Unscrupulous landlords charge huge rents. Sometimes 20 or 25 people must live in one room. With no right to work, some factories prosper on their cheap labour.'

Many refugees came from educated backgrounds, and the dramatic drop in their standard of living, compounded by the difficulties of their immigrant status, could be so shocking, he continued, that even those 'who arrive determined to somehow make a better life for themselves and their families spiral down into hopelessness'.

Accidentally Istanbul

But there were success stories. The day came when an Iranian student of mine, 13-year-old Kimiyah and her 16-year-old brother were leaving. They had found a sponsor in Canada. At a small farewell ceremony at the school, the girl's father was jubilant, if nervous. 'When we left Iran we didn't know what a pit we were falling into,' he told me. He had been a 747 airline captain in Iran. Suddenly, his wife was under suspicion of being a covert Christian: 'the wrong person saw a book she was reading, which had been in her grandfather's library'. Its theme was comparative religions. Twenty-four hours later he and his family took a flight to Turkey.

'We knew right away that we had to act quickly. We had seen what had happened to other families. We collected the children from school, took no clothes, what little money we could get together without drawing attention to ourselves, and raced to the airport.'

His face showed the pain of leaving his parents and siblings behind. Four difficult years had ensued, with no recognition of their claim by the UNHCR.

'We need a country,' he confided earnestly. 'We want to have something for our children, a good life without fear.'

I was overjoyed for them, if very sad to see Kimiyah leave. She had been a keen student, intelligent, loving her schooling, always doing more homework than she was given. We hugged continually on that last day. As they were leaving, she ran back for just one more hug. I knew, and I think she knew too, that

Accidentally Istanbul

we would probably never see one another again.

But the thing that touched me most, that still stays with me today, was the reaction of Talya. While we all stood watching and waving on the church porch, and I stood at the back, trying to smile, but swallowing and holding my breath a little, the family walked out the church gate for the last time. At that moment I felt a rush of small arms around my waist. It was Talya, trying to share comfort with her own small embrace.

Kimiyah was immediately replaced by another student (there was a long waiting list) and I began another small relationship. And so it went on. Talya and others like her cheerfully took what they could get at the refugee school, because there was nothing else. And they waited.

Every story was different. One afternoon, I had reason to pass through a pleasant courtyard in central Istanbul. Here I found a scattered crowd of Africans, their parted and braided hair gleaming in the sunshine. They were waiting for medical attention. The doctors were refugees themselves. The Somali translator was the father of another former student. His smile was generous in his big face, he laughed often, and his eyes shone with quick intelligence.

'We had to leave Somalia,' he told me as he waited to be called to interpret. 'It was too dangerous.' He explained that he'd witnessed a murder and was frightened for his life, as well as for his family's wellbeing. He had paid US$4500 to smugglers for a trip to Italy by ship. It took the family to a beach in the middle

Accidentally Istanbul

of the night. 'This is Italy,' they had said, dropping his family and others in shallow water.

But it was Turkey. And here they remained, having been turned down for refugee status. He said he had twice paid smugglers to take his family overland into Greece. Both attempts had been unsuccessful. 'So we stay here. Eight years now, and a new baby. But what can we do?'

Later I talked to another Istanbul woman, a co-ordinator for the IIMP which finds sponsors in Western countries to help settle refugee families. She thought that the West was closing its doors against people like this man.

'A big majority of these asylum-seekers are the cream of the crop, you know,' she said, sadly. 'They're the hard workers, the deserving. All they need is the chance to start again without fear, in freedom.'

This was becoming more than a volunteer job for me. Every day I began to identify more strongly with the plight of the families whose children I taught. Never in my life could I remember feeling so *necessary*.

But it was also very confusing. In daylight hours I was busy. But it was at night, with too much time to think, and in my dreams, that I was disturbed. It was as if my life's edifice was crumbling. Australia seemed very far away at these moments. I had trouble remembering the person I had been, with a circle of responsibilities, friends and a family I loved. I had thought I had led a good life, caring for my kids, working for them, giving them a carefree childhood. Now I had quick moments of shame, shame that the love I extended to family and friends was not *enough*.

In the meantime, twice each week, Talya and others like her cheerfully came to school and I equally cheerfully gave what I could. But sometimes I would find myself weeping as I made my way home, staring out the bus window to hide my tears. Yet there was also another me, staring into the window, and she was saying: *Why are you crying? It's not your problem. This is not your country. You're Australian and you don't have to get upset about kids who are strangers in the country in which you're a stranger yourself. You're being crazy, Nancy.*

But was I?

15

Headscarves

'Look, Ted, the girl on our right … No—don't look like that!'
'But you told me to look …'
We were sitting on a bus on our way into town.
I took a quick breath. 'Yes, but *discreetly*.'
He turned to me with a grin. We were used to being able to talk on buses in English without anyone understanding. After a pause, during which I fumed a little, he said: 'OK, I've looked discreetly. What about her?'
'When I see someone like her, it always seems so odd—a bare midriff, a ring in her navel and a flowered headscarf covering her head.'
He laughed. 'Well yes, I did notice the—ah—navel.'
'But then covering up with a headscarf? Isn't that weird?'
'Mmmm, maybe.' But he was already staring out the window.

Accidentally Istanbul

I retreated into my own thoughts.

Since our arrival in Istanbul I had been both captivated and disquieted by headscarves—or the lack of them. Captivated by the vibrant colours that enlivened the streets, disquieted because I didn't understand what made some women wear them and others not. In those early months we were seeing through a blurred glass of naïveté, observing closely but without even the tiniest understanding.

I continued to watch the headscarf-wearers, and my interest increased until it was verging on obsession. There were so many different versions. Mothers wore headscarves while their daughters wore multiple rings in their ears, too much make-up, and bared navels above the tightest of jeans. What passed between these mothers and daughters? How much did the conversation relate to religion?

I turned as ever to books. The history was fascinating.

The *fez*, the male head-dress, the typical symbol of Islamic orthodoxy in the Ottoman era, was frowned upon by Ataturk, who was intent on making Turkey into 'a civilised nation'. The *fez* was therefore arbitrarily banned by the passing of the Hat Law, passed in 1925 by the National Assembly. The tradition of women wearing 'the veil' as it was called at the time, was not banned. However Ataturk's then-wife, Latife Uşakizade, discarded it herself and encouraged all other women to do the same.

It was not until 1997, with the ousting of an Islamic-leaning government by the military, that headscarves were banned by

Accidentally Istanbul

the new government in all public institutions.

The current conservative government, led by the outspoken and articulate Recep Tayyip Erdoğan had, as I've noted, a core constituency of religious voters, mostly poor people in rural areas. Educated secularists feared Islamisation under Erdoğan's AK Party and headscarves seemed to have assumed enhanced symbolic and political status.

Erdoğan's wife, Emine, wore a headscarf, unusual even for the wives of much more conservative Middle Eastern states. We saw a newspaper photo one day of the Erdoğans with the heads of state and their wives of most of the Arab countries, from Saudi Arabia to Jordan, from Syria to Iran.

Mrs Erdoğan was the only one wearing a headscarf.

In the universities, where headscarves were banned, and in the wealthy suburbs, one hardly ever saw a covered head. In the trendy coffee houses, including Starbucks and Gloria Jean's, you were no more likely to see a headscarf than in Sydney's Paddington. To many secular Turks the headscarf was simply a sign of backwardness, whereas to others, equally secular, the right of the individual to freedom of religion and dress was seen as paramount.

I was mischievously amused by the thought that while the headscarf had become a political issue, no-one ever suggested that Turkish men return to wearing the *fez*.

Now Ted's voice interrupted my reverie. 'So are you going to tell me something about Miss Ringed Navel?'

'If she's religious enough to wear a headscarf, how come

Accidentally Istanbul

she's wearing skin-tight hipster jeans and a ring in her navel? It doesn't make sense.'

In 2005, bare midriffs were the current Western rage. 'Most of the girls in my classes show midriffs and at least half of them have navel rings.' Ted flashed a smile in my direction. 'It's very hard to know where to look!'

I had always been a keen people-watcher, and I now privately separated Istanbul's head-scarfed women into categories. First was the traditional older woman who tied it under her chin. This blended with her sturdy walking shoes and long jumper hanging unevenly around her usually ample body. The colours were patterned browns, creams, soft greens or beige. The scarf flowed naturally down her back, as unobtrusive as a quiet bush stream.

However, many a young woman with her would be in a miniskirt, or with a bare midriff or in jeans, sweatshirt and runners. She might be chewing gum, sporting big loop earrings and have her iPod clamped into her ears.

Other young women, often with mothers, were traditionally dressed, inexpensively and unobtrusively. Their eyes were averted, hands folded diffidently on laps or clasped shyly around a shoulder bag. They were usually pale of countenance and always unadorned: good, dutiful children, not rebelling by following flashy ways. I was told that in conservative circles a 'good Muslim woman' will not smile or meet the eyes of strangers in public. This is crass, unladylike behaviour.

Accidentally Istanbul

In addition, among the throbbing crowds of this vast city, there were the wonderful head-dresses of up-country women who wore lace-bordered white scarves swathed around their temples. They wore the traditional colourful baggy pants and flowing garments of their regions.

The least easy for me to understand were the black-robed women with only their eyes visible. Some were visiting Saudi Arabian holiday makers, but if Turkish, I was told, they belonged to religious cults, and were often those at the edge of their society and drawn by loneliness.

But what about those such as the girl on the bus? There seemed something forced and self-conscious about them. What they were thinking? Their scarves were wild oranges, electric greens, bright sky blues, boldly patterned, bouncing like flowers in windy grass. The shape was curious. The scarf rose smoothly like a beehive or an Egyptian queen's head-dress, suggesting a head of unnatural shape. They were bright-eyed, these young women, faces made up to perfection, their walk confident, their manner haughty. They *never* gave up their seats on buses to the old or the frail. I called them Princesses of Turkey: confident, insolent, superior.

What were the messages from these different modes of dress? How much was religion, how much was politics and how much custom?

I started, diffidently at first, to ask questions of anyone who would listen. I began to welcome opportunities to talk to people.

Accidentally Istanbul

Instead of merely dismissing it as something mysterious to the Western mind, I extended my informal survey to taxi drivers, market-stall holders and university students, but it seemed almost impossible to actually talk with scarf-wearing women. It was difficult to find any who admitted to speaking English.

Finally a complex picture began to emerge from the cacophony of voices gathered in my head.

My private student Doğan was a university graduate and successful accountant. His English was flawed but flowing, so our lessons consisted of philosophical or political conversations, while I corrected his syntax and grammar. Proud that he was hard-working, self-made and affluent, he displayed an erudite knowledge of the history and politics of Turkey and Europe.

He and his family were agnostic by belief but, naturally, Muslim by tradition.

'My sister-in-law—she's mad. My wife and her sister, they came from an educated home and didn't wear headscarves.'

Ah, so you equate headscarves with lack of education ...

'Then when she married her husband, he said: "You can do what you like, but I'm telling you, not to wear a headscarf is a sin."'

A sin? Do they use that word or was that for my sake?

'So now she wears it! And their only son, who is extremely intelligent and could do anything that he wants, is sent to religious school where all they learn is Koran, Koran, Koran. Crazy! They are mad, that family. And when I say to them: "Why don't you educate your son properly? It's not fair to him," he says "If he has a good religious education, God will look after him."'

Doğan was despairing. Even his wife, he said, now saw her sister only on family occasions. It made me remember Australian families similarly divided because of intermarriage between Christian denominations. I was cracking the egg.

Then there was Emine, whom I met on a bus one day. I had helped her get off with her pram, and then we chatted briefly. I said that since we were almost neighbours, we should meet one day, and she agreed, shyly but enthusiastically.

We both arrived on time and sat drinking tea in a simple teagarden at the end of our street. Her English was halting, limited (I guessed) to lessons at school.

She was again wearing a headscarf. She was well-dressed, sleek pants suit, modern and complicated pram. Her friend, Arzu, a little older and speaking no English, had come with her (*for protection? for moral support?*). Arzu's children were at school, she told me in Turkish, with a broad, proud smile. My Turkish was improving and I could now manage simple conversations.

Emine's headscarf was more colourful than Arzu's, and, rather than flowing freely, was tucked in at the collar. I took in these differences quickly as we were greeting one another. Her friend was carefully dressed too, and showed signs of wanting to be trendy: she was completely clothed in denim. However, instead of the ubiquitous jeans worn by all her non-headscarfed contemporaries, she wore a denim skirt to the ground, covered

Accidentally Istanbul

by a denim coat to the knees.

Hers was an arranged marriage, Emine told me, in the sense that the families had spoken before the children met. 'But if I did not like him, my family would not have made me marry him,' she told me.

Emine told me she always wore a headscarf. 'It is God's law even though my father does not go to the mosque—so you could not say we are a religious family.' She became thoughtful as we waited for coffee to arrive. 'You know, in our village near Eskişehir it is good—respectable [she stumbled over the word]—for a woman to have her head covered. I have never thought of not doing it. I didn't go to university, so no-one expected me to take off my headscarf. I am very happy wearing it. I would feel uncomfortable without it.'

'And your husband?'

'My husband?'

'Does he want you to wear a headscarf?'

'Yes,' she said simply.

She seemed a passive soul, completely taken up with her baby. She bent over to wipe his mouth carefully. Then, without warning or explanation, she said: 'I am very lucky that my husband is a kind and respectable man.' I could feel a torrent of unsaid sentiments hiding in this innocuous remark, but was loath to press further.

We enjoyed the sunshine and talked about her baby and Arzu's two children. As I returned home I was anything but sure that I had penetrated these young women's real feelings.

Some of the other young women who wore headscarves did not show Emine's natural manner. Often I failed when I tried to start up casual conversations, but at a morning opening of an art gallery exhibition, I watched a girl across the room. She looked a sweet child, maybe 18, with clear skin and dark shining eyes. Her headscarf was a fresh blue-and-white flower pattern, teaming nicely with her long white coat and sky-blue floor-length skirt—but it seemed to be covering a beehive hairdo. She was coquettish, as many Turkish girls are, simpering and giggling with her group, affected in a charming naïve way. In the crush we bumped into one another and exchanged smiles, so I grabbed the chance to make a comment about the paintings to start a conversation.

Her name, I discovered, was Meltem. She was delighted to practise her English and allowed her friends to drift off while we shared information with one another. I admired her headscarf and her clothes as nonchalantly as I could. Then she talked about what covered her head. 'I'm not normally allowed to wear this at university, and I didn't wear one when I was younger, but now many of my friends like to wear the headscarf.'

'It's very pretty,' I said. 'But tell me,' as I leant forward confidentially, 'how do you make it stay in that lovely beehive shape?' She stumbled a little as if she didn't know what I meant by 'beehive shape', but finally understood my question. She giggled. 'It's a kind of wire net— you know, to keep my scarf straight.'

Accidentally Istanbul

She was not religious (*or was that merely for my benefit?*) and I deduced from our conversation that she was wearing her headscarf merely as a fashion accessory.

The most telling of my conversations was with two older women journalists, long-time political observers. We had coffee in a place close to our apartment block. One of the women wrote a widely-read and often controversial column. Since I knew I would feel confident communicating with such a worldly journalist, I had boldly phoned her, asking if we could meet. She had agreed gladly, and brought her friend. But when I told them that I might write about what they said, they quickly stipulated anonymity.

These two were urban sophisticates, hair well-coiffed, minimal make-up, nails painted. Their English was fluent and idiomatic and everything about their manner Western. 'I lived for many years in California,' said the friend.

'You see, headscarves are a subject that we cannot discuss very much—not frankly. It's dangerous. You remember Salman Rushdie? These people are very dangerous, so it's best to keep to safe subjects.'

When I asked why women wore scarves, their tone became patronising. 'Oh, there are so many reasons why these women wear them. It's mostly about power.'

'Power?' I echoed.

'Yes—power.'

She mentioned the name of a well-known politician's wife.

Accidentally Istanbul

'She didn't wear a headscarf when she was young, but then her brother joined some kind of movement and he beat her up. So since then she has had to wear the headscarf. That's the power of the Family. Then there is the power of the Man, the Husband. She is a possession, his woman. He wants to appear in charge, and he wants the world to know that his wife is a good moral woman and under his control.

'Then there's the power of Fashion. Some of these silly girls do it to be stylish. It's a modern fashion now. Wearing headscarves has increased in the last few years. Did you know that?' (*Ah, so that could have been the case with the girl at the gallery.*)

'So an increase in the wearing of headscarves doesn't necessarily signify an increase in religious fervour?'

She gave a low laugh, almost a snicker. She didn't answer my question, but continued, caught up in her own momentum.

'Then, there's the power of Laziness—'

'Laziness?' I was surprised.

'Yes, of course. Don't you think it's easier to get up in the morning and tie a scarf around your head and call it religion? I know women who are too damned lazy to bother. Look at all the trouble we go to in maintaining our hairdos: primping and preening, going to the hairdresser and paying a fortune. If you just tie the whole lot up in a scarf you don't have to worry about all that nonsense.'

'Not a bad idea,' laughed her friend.

'Well don't take to wearing one, dear—or you can have coffee

Accidentally Istanbul

with someone else.'

They were a ribald pair, and fun to be with. No sacred cows for them.

'But you have to understand the agenda.' The woman leant back slowly in the booth, and gave me a serious look. 'This government is encouraging the wearing of headscarves. They want to change the status quo from Ataturk's vision. They're playing a double game, encouraging the association with the European Union to weaken the power of the military in Turkey. Once that power is undermined, then they can turn us back into an Islamic state.'

This was the prevailing local conspiracy theory that I had heard described so many times before.

'Do you really believe that?' They exchanged knowing smiles and the subject was changed. Some things were clearly too dangerous to discuss. Our conversation lightened as we moved on to other subjects.

Their words continued to echo in my head, ricocheting, demanding my attention without warning: conspiracies, secret political agendas, the power of Laziness, of the Husband, the Family.

That evening, as I considered it all, Ted asked: 'Did you hear what I said?'

'Oh yes—I mean no. Sorry, what did you say, Ted?'

'I said Irem just called. They want to have dinner somewhere in Nevizade Sokak.'

Accidentally Istanbul

'Fine. Great.'

This society had so many layers, I was finding—yet more than mere layers. There was such cross-fertilisation of ideas and tradition and religion and political thought that to try and separate them all was a gargantuan, if not impossible task. Definitions slipped away like a mirage. One minute I would think I understood, then the next confusion reigned again. I sighed as I grappled with the slippery truths I was hearing. Maybe I would never completely 'understand', but then maybe there were as many truths flying around this city and hovering around its laneways as there were minds to decipher them and tongues to express them. My diving into the vast seas of changing Turkish culture by turn exhilarated, distressed and soothed me. As I swam I was, increasingly, strangely refreshed by my immersion in these strong currents.

16

The multipurpose repairman

We gradually, gradually learned how to look after ourselves: find the best supermarket, where to have shoes repaired and where to buy household utensils. I always enjoyed learning more Turkish words. Ted was content to stay silent as shopkeepers broke into laughter at my super-serious attempts to use their language.

Gül remained a vital aide. While our apartment appeared quite swish on the surface, as time passed we discovered both comical and serious defects. The light switches were wired back-to-front so that the hall switch turned on the kitchen light and vice versa. The glamorous black-marbled bathroom seeped water and the television set was cantankerous and unreliable.

I started with the bathroom leaks. Gül organised a plumber

Accidentally Istanbul

and he appeared at the door one morning with a professional-looking metal case of tools. He was a genial young man, handsome, polite and with a small number of English words at his disposal. Like all Turkish workmen, he walked out of his shoes at the door in a single movement and worked in his socks. When he found he needed some extra pipes, he left indicating he would be back *yarin*, tomorrow.

We were both delighted with his speed and professionalism.

Sure enough he was back on cue the next day, after Ted had left for the University, to complete the job, cleaning the bathroom meticulously once he had finished. Then, hoping I could avoid troubling Gül with every small problem, I asked him, half in English, half in Turkish, if he had a friend who was an electrician.

'What is the problem?' he asked in Turkish. Not being able to explain, I showed him the lights which were not working. '*Problem yok* (no problem),' he said instantly, and smilingly disappeared out the door again.

I went on preparing the lesson I was to give that afternoon, assuming he was going to contact his electrician friend. However, five minutes later he reappeared at the door with a different case of tools, sporting a big smile and, shoes off, headed for the fuse box.

'*You* are an electrician too?' I said in English, amazed.

'*Problem yok*,' he kept repeating, and set about attending to my faulty switches. Then, even more amazing, when I asked him, he set about fixing the television set. It appeared there was

Accidentally Istanbul

nothing this young man couldn't do! I was stunned and he was clearly delighted in my surprise at his multifarious skills.

He was still working when Ted came blowing in like a fresh wind, buoyed by his day at the University and unusually chatty. He went into his office to open his emails.

I had forgotten to warn him. Soon I could hear 'What the ...?' followed by some soft but decidedly ungodly expletives.

He appeared, framed in the doorway, as though he had seen a ghost.

'You have the *plumber* fixing the television set?'

'Yes—he insisted he could. He also fixed the faulty lights in the back room and replaced some of the wiring."

'Are you crazy? Do you want to burn the building down? And how do you know he won't wreck the set?'

He turned to thunder back down the hall.

'Ted, don't do anything,' I called. 'Gül arranged him. He must be all right.'

I caught him by the sleeve just as he seemed about to hurl himself bodily between the plumber/electrician/television-repairman and the set he was busily fixing.

'Let's go and ask Gül. Now. Before you say anything to him.'

The multitalented workman had simply reacted by looking up and smiling as he continued to turn a screwdriver in the bowels of the television set.

I dragged a reluctant Ted away to cross the landing to knock loudly on Gül's door. We must have looked alarmed as she

Accidentally Istanbul

opened it, apron on, her vast, comfortable smile at the ready. At the sight of her I could feel Ted's alarm dissipate, his tension slip away.

I asked Gül slowly, in my halting Turkish, if this man she had recommended as a good plumber was also skilled at electrical work and television repairs. Welcoming as always, she nodded, he was indeed *iyi*, good.

'Electrical *iyi*?' I insisted.

'*Evet* (yes),' she said, nodding.

'TV *iyi*?' I persisted.

Now she was smiling and shrugging, a little mystified, but agreed that he was a good, good workman.

Ted was not a happy man but, charmed by Gül's breezy confidence, agreed much against his better judgement, not to evict our very flexible handyman.

It was later explained by other foreigners that qualifications do not count for much and Turkey does not control licences for such workmen. This also illustrated to us why, when we walked through Istanbul, thousands of electrical cables looped over buildings, were strung across streets in crazy patterns and hung precariously like mad spiders' webs down back walls. The city hangs together with jury-rigged wiring and very creative plumbing configurations.

After the young repairman's visit, the pipes did not leak and all the lights responded to their correct switches. Before he left, our man had showed us where the faulty connection was and

Accidentally Istanbul

how to fix it—that is, he showed me as Ted stood by, hands shoved into pockets, scowling and muttering that the female mafia (Gül and I) were taking over the world.

Reminding him that he was getting Turkey mixed up with Italy didn't lift his mood.

There were other, greater, differences in maintenance regimes between our countries. Turkey had not yet reached the casual 'throw-away' consumer society we knew. In Australia I was used to a response that went: 'We can't get parts for these any more. You're better off not wasting your money. We can sell you a new one.'

In Turkey, broken-down refrigerators, stoves, pipes, taps or any other household items were laboriously repaired. If no part was available, the workman simply went away to have it made by a one-man operation with a large metal-working lathe. Items were repaired and repaired again. Tradesman usually didn't speak any English, the negotiation happened with smiling, nodding and my humorous infantile Turkish, then the handing over of very, very small sums of money.

Now our time passed into a happy routine. The weather cooled and soon lovely grey, misty mornings gave way reluctantly to the sun. A pigeon often sat on my windowsill, its tail blowing sideways in the wind. In the light-wells between the apartments I could hear the birds cooing in their nests. The sound was intimate, the unseen homely lives of birds going about their business. These moments were cosy, warming to the soul.

Accidentally Istanbul

As we breakfasted each day by the window and the weather freshened, we would watch the pedestrians below bent forward in their leather coats. Some days seagulls collected on the grass of the sportsfield across the road, quite a reliable forecast, we came to realise, of bad weather approaching. Inside the apartment, the maze of gentle central heating pipes kept us snug, and the sunshine streamed in on one side of the flat or the other, morning and afternoon.

Meanwhile, CNN, Al Jazeera, BBC News and Euronews, the television channels we had access to because they were in English, went on and on about the Iraq War and the death of Yasir Arafat.

Our lives were led as in a bubble. Inside our comfortable flat we were like any Australian family: Vegemite for breakfast, a roast once a week. Outside the bubble there was the new world to explore. We discovered that the streets— any street— seemed to be safe for walking at all times of the day or night. As a result we became more and more relaxed about venturing into unknown areas. *Unlike Sydney*, I couldn't help thinking, remembering the cinema end of George Street on weekend nights.

Occasionally during our peregrinations, Ted would stop suddenly grab me into a bear hug and whisper, mocking an Australian country radio program, *Australia All Over*: 'Well, Oy *love* it!'

I too started to love our adventures into unknown suburbs

Accidentally Istanbul

and corners of the huge city. The contrasts of tradition and modernity were a constant stimulation to our senses. Next to trendy warehouse conversions on the foreshore were 1000-year-old ruins, grey and forbidding. Among the tall sky-cutting modern blue glass towers were the softly swooping lines of cupolas and minarets.

And the citizens! Used to our own comparatively egalitarian community, the variations were forever exotic to my eye. The contrast between most modern glamorous and fashionable young women against those covered in black except for their eyes was constantly disturbing. I still couldn't help thinking: *What do they think of one another?* Round the corner from the most stylish restaurants, patronised by blonde-streaked beauties who stepped out of Porsches clad in the latest Armani gear, you could find little alleyways full of handiwork spread on trestle tables and simply-aproned stallholders who muttered the untranslatable *Buyurun* in a quiet plea for custom. Exquisite jewellery could be had for a dollar or two.

How did they all live together so placidly? The culture was an enigma, as if written in a secret code. How could I ever decipher it in the time we had left?

We were adjusting in a superficial way to our new-found lives, but often Ted and I still shook our heads in disbelief. We (I laugh at my use of 'we' meaning 'we in Turkey') seemed to be at the intersection of so many levels of world politics, constantly in the headlines of Western newspapers and television. As a vital link between European and Middle Eastern politics; as the recipient of acts of violence from rebellious Kurds wanting a Kurdistan of their own; on the defence against the Armenian massacre accusations; or sometimes as a separate voice on the already-growing divide between the West and Islam, Turkey seemed to be where realpolitik was playing itself out.

The Turk in the street, unlike the average Australian, was vocally and proudly Turkish. On any public celebration day, flags of incredible size hung from office buildings as though all were in competition to see who could produce the largest. Some stretched the full width of the building and hung down several storeys. Many homes flew their own flags too and the tops of buildings were similarly garlanded.

The way forward into the EU seemed anything but clear. Every negative comment by Europeans about Turkey's potential entry burst into headlines in the Turkish press. We followed the endless discussions: claims that Turkish is not a European language, ignoring its linguistic relationships to Hungarian and Finnish, countries already in the EU; or that the European part of Turkey occupied only 3 per cent of the country, a strange argument given that member Cyprus lies closer to the Middle East than Turkey and south of the Arab country of Tunisia.

Lurking in the muddy waters below these claims were (never mentioned) suspicions of racism and religious exclusivity. Turkey's past human rights record during its tumultuous history, from the Armenian genocide to its record of torture

Accidentally Istanbul

and hanging of political losers, was another unstated barrier. As the weeks went by, we read of the passing of much legislation to 'correct' some of the 'problem' areas. Kurdish language radio stations flourished, jailed dissidents were released and the power of the military dwindled.

Seen in the light of events still to come, this furore seems almost comical, but all these topics were the subject of debate and passionate disagreement around the coffee tables of Istanbul. Every time we met people, Turkish or foreigners, the EU was the top subject. Should we join or not? How valid were the arguments of Europeans? Were they just a cover for not wanting a Muslim country to join? Everyone had an opinion and no one could have guessed how redundant these argument would become as the Global Financial Crisis struck and Europe sank to new lows while Turkey continued to prosper.

Not only the GFC, but also the death of Osama Bin Laden, the spread of conflicts between Shiites and Sunni Muslims, the Arab Spring, the political volcano that has engulfed the Arab world—all these were still to come.

'I know what the answer is,' said Ted triumphantly as we returned home one evening from dinner with friends. 'Turkey doesn't really want to be in the EU—but they do want to be *invited.*'

I laughed, thinking this wasn't so ridiculous. There seemed to be a schizophrenic thread in all the debates. Those who declared themselves against joining the EU often then spent

Accidentally Istanbul

time damning the reasons Europeans were against it.

What Turkey wanted next was a timetable for accession talks, but this was not forthcoming. To add insult to injury, the issue of Cyprus, that small island now divided between Greeks and Turks, constantly stood in the way. 'Greek' Cyprus became a member of the EU, leaving 'Turkish' Cyprus feeling isolated and ignored by the world community.

Tomorrow was always a puzzle—but also an exciting prospect.

At moments I had stabs of regret. Keen as I was to leave at the end of the winter semester, it would be like stopping an engrossing novel when you were only halfway through.

There were other matters to regret, too. I was so enjoying learning Turkish. I was just getting to know Gül, whose friendship I was starting to treasure, as well as that of the others, both Western and Turkish. We hadn't seen Kapadokia with its fairy chimneys; or amazing rock-built Mardin on the Tigris River, where they still spoke the language of Jesus Christ in fourth-century churches; or Pamukkale, Cotton Castle, with its hot springs and sparkling white mineral terraces. We hadn't even been to Gallipoli.

Would I only ever know these places through pictures? Their images came to me in flashes late at night, like a collage, waking me with feelings of things lost: faces, places, words. Confused in the dark, I tossed and turned in rumpled sheets, while Ted slept soundly and quietly beside me, supremely unaware of my sense of regret at a loss yet to come.

17

Turkish eyes

There was so much more to discover—and discover it we did, little by little, day by day. Occasionally in the bazaars we met someone who spoke enough English to have a conversation. This was the case with the Turkish Eye. These are always made of glass and always blue. We often heard tourists ask for the 'Evil Eye'.

One old bazaar vendor watched me fingering one, loving the smooth, cool feel of the glass, the pureness of the blue. He leant forward conspiratorially.

'In the olden days in Turkey …' he began, launching into surprisingly good English, 'when wolves were still a threat, the people feared them because they were always hungry in winter. They would creep into the houses and carry away small children.'

My eyes were wide with disbelief.

Accidentally Istanbul

'They were very dangerous and everyone was frightened of them.'

I remembered Red Riding Hood and Goldilocks, the bloodthirsty stories of my childhood. Maybe they weren't so far-fetched. But in my own childhood in Far North Queensland, taipans and crocodiles were the real danger. It seemed ironic that all the scary fairy tales had been about wolves and bears.

The old man was still talking, still leaning forward, interrupting my reverie. 'Wolves have very good eyesight, you see, so if they saw an adult in the window they would be too frightened to enter a house. So the people started to paint big eyes on their windows, to make them think *a very big person* was watching them. The *Nazar Boncuk*, the Turkish Eye, was originally for this purpose.'

'Really!' Now I was fascinated.

He straightened up, laughing. 'But don't worry—today there are only wolves in the far regions of Turkey and the houses are built more strongly. So now it's just a good luck charm to keep away evil.'

I started to thank him and prepare to buy some Turkish Eyes. But he hadn't finished.

'You must buy these for your friends, not for you. It's always better when an Eye is given as a gift; the charm works better. So let someone else buy a Turkish Eye and give it to you.'

By now I was entranced. I started to open my wallet—but he started speaking again.

'When you hang this Turkish Eye, you must put it at the

Accidentally Istanbul

entrance to your house, nowhere else. In this way all evil, not just the evil of wolves, will be kept from your door. Even better, set it in the stone of the doorstep so that to enter the house you must walk over it. This is the very best of all!'

We laughed and I bought many more Turkish Eyes than intended. Did I believe his story of the wolves? I wasn't sure. He was either a very good salesman or for him it was the truth. And I wanted to believe it too.

One day not long after this encounter, I was in a pharmacy where people were coming and going, chatting and smiling. I waited my turn, smiling and nodding when anyone looked in my direction. The smiles were returned, except by one elderly head-scarfed woman. She sat on a chair in a corner in brown, shapeless clothing, a large dull-coloured fabric bag beside her on the floor. Her head was kept bowed, but occasionally she glanced up and scowled at me, then looked away, sour-faced. Her eyes were dark and sunk far into her face, glistening black set in wrinkled brown skin. She had a large bulbous nose, so that even with her head bowed it showed in profile.

The pharmacist was a glamorous middle-aged woman, hair elegantly blonde-streaked, make-up perfect and speaking excellent English. I noticed that she was drinking hot tea with a small branch floating in it.

I was curious. 'What kind of tea is that?'

'It's *ada çayı* (she said *arda chay*). That means 'island tea. It's very good for colds and flu. It's a little like sage.'

Accidentally Istanbul

'How interesting. Can I buy some?'

The pharmacist lifted her chin a little, in the signal for *no*, and laughed. 'No no—you can't buy it here. We wouldn't sell such things. Next time you go to the bazaar, maybe they have some there. But let me give you some of mine.'

I protested, but she had already reached into a drawer and was putting some in a paper bag. 'Just drop it into boiling water. It's *so* good if you have a cold.'

Then the grim old woman suddenly began to speak. Her voice was old but strong. Her words were addressed to the pharmacist and although she didn't once look at me, I could tell by her reactions, as she glanced continually at me, that I was the subject of their conversation.

Then an amazing thing happened. The old woman's entire personality seemed to change. Her face creased into a wreath of smiles. Her wrinkled eyes twinkled and her face, so dour before, glowed with animation. She spoke to me rapidly in Turkish. The pharmacist tried to translate, but the woman was speaking so fast she stopped, laughing, raising both hands in mock-frustration, shaking her head.

She told me the old woman was talking about *ada çayı*, explaining that where she lived she had to crawl down the cliffs beside the sea to collect it. This was very precarious, and her arthritis was troubling, so sometimes her son visited and he collected it for her. She went on talking while the pharmacist smiled indulgently, translating in summary fashion.

Accidentally Istanbul

I nodded and smiled, taken aback at this change of mood.

Then the old woman was scrabbling in her large bag. From it she produced some walnuts still in their shell. She thrust them at me, hauling out more and more, and the pharmacist, still amused, quickly offered another paper bag to hold them.

'She's saying that she grows these walnuts on her farm and they are very, very healthy, very good for you, just like *ada çayı*. She is wishing you good health.'

I left the pharmacy burdened with these gifts: a large bag of tea and another of walnuts. I was so moved by the generosity of both educated sophisticate and villager, but mystified by the old woman's original attitude.

A new Turkish friend had an immediate solution. 'She wasn't disapproving, just shy. Some of these people live such isolated lives that simply coming into town is stressful. To be faced with a *yabancı*, a foreigner, would have been quite frightening. However, once you became human—someone happy to drink Turkish *ada çayı*, she saw you as just another person like she is.'

My friend grinned. 'She'll be telling her neighbours all week about meeting you.'

It wasn't about me, not about me: my heart sang a glad, sad little song. Even in sophisticated Istanbul, people living traditional lives were never far away. A desire for connection hung around me like a mist for the rest of the day. I couldn't get the old woman out of my mind.

18

Ramazan

Suddenly everyone was talking about Ramazan, the Turkish word for Ramadan. We understood little about it, but knew that it was the month of fasting, reminding me of the 40 days of Lent. Ramazan fasting is usually 30 days and the timing is based on the moon, so the dates vary every year, just like Easter, except they constantly move earlier instead of hovering around March and April.

The reason for Ramazan is also a little like Lent, but the regime is much more severe. In traditional Islam, all adults are expected to fast during daylight hours, and many (but by no means all) in Turkey do. This makes for some extraordinary behaviour. For instance, breakfast must occur before daylight. After fasting all day (including no water), at sundown they participate in *Iftar*, the celebratory end of the daily fast. Even

Accidentally Istanbul

those who don't fast still enjoy the observance of *Iftar* with their families, just as atheists still take Christmas holidays to spend time with family.

Fasting all day tends to cause irritation and lack of concentration as sunset draws near. I read in the newspapers that educators and health experts were campaigning to have water excluded from the fast. The teachers at Berlitz warned me, saying that lessons between 5 and 8pm could be a disaster, since for the first hour the students were irritable and lacked concentration. At the half-time break, after sunset, they gorged themselves with food and then, complained my teacher friends, went to sleep for the second half of the lesson.

Many others observed Ramazan in a token gesture, by giving up chocolate, or some other nominated item—certainly not water. Nilufer, a beautiful young student friend, simply gave up wine. Again I was reminded of Lent. 'What are you giving up for Lent?' was our question to one another when I was a child at Sunday School.

The city buzzed with excitement as the end of Ramazan approached, as everyone prepared for the three-day *Bayramı* or holiday, sometimes called the Sugar Holiday (*Şeker Bayramı*). I was told it took its name from the tradition of children knocking on neighbourhood doors and receiving sweets, much like the American Halloween, but without the 'tricks'. On the last day of the month-long fast there was a huge exodus from the city, all heading home to visit distant families.

Accidentally Istanbul

During our first Ramazan we were invited to spend a weekend at Gül and Şeref's holiday house at Silivri on the Sea of Marmara. Since they spoke no English and my Turkish was still very limited, this promised to be quite a challenge, but we set off in their car on the Saturday after Şeref finished work at midday, Saturday morning work being the rule rather than the exception.

Gül and Şeref sat in the front, while 17-year-old Fehmi, Ted and I packed into the back. Their holiday house was in a coastal development, very prettily arranged and with repetitive house designs. They proudly took us for a walk around the complex, including a golf course, a swimming pool and tennis courts. All were deserted.

Gül and Fehmi both had a blood-type that allowed them to avoid Ramazan fasting, so lunch was taken without Şeref, who repaired to his bedroom. Late flowers bloomed in the garden beside us as we ate, watching their cat fight imaginary mice in the garden beds.

As soon as we finished eating, Şeref joined us and Gül excitedly walked us through the garden to show off the rare roses she grew. Living as they did in an Istanbul apartment, this house and garden allowed them to indulge in the pleasures of gardening, as well as eating outdoors. Gül also had a vegetable garden and fruit trees. *So this was where all my presents originated.*

It was a quiet weekend, a time of friendship, but the most memorable part was the breaking of Şeref's fast.

Accidentally Istanbul

As evening drew near we took our places in the living-dining room as if a momentous occasion was imminent. For Şeref, who had eaten and drunk nothing since before daylight, it no doubt *was* momentous. The evening meal, dates, salads, vegetable dishes, pastry triangles, *simit* and *köfte* and other foods I didn't recognise, were laid out on the table in splendid array.

The television was, surprisingly, turned on just as we were about to eat. Gradually the reason became clear. A special TV channel recorded the exact moment at which the sun set for all the towns and cities in Turkey. Because Istanbul was east of Silivri, Şeref would have to wait longer than someone back in the city. On the screen we watched the towns and cities rolling through, lighting up when it was time to eat in that zone.

We sat feeling Şeref's tense expectation as we watched the small greyed-out town of Silivri gradually making its way up the list on the screen. Finally its lights started flashing and, with a great sigh, Şeref slowly and carefully reached for a long glass of water which Gül had waiting for him. He drank slowly, smiled at us with infinite calm, took some dates in a very measured fashion from a small bowl at his elbow, and we all began our meal together.

When we woke the next morning, Gül and Fehmi were waiting to have breakfast but Şeref had breakfasted before dawn and then returned to bed to read the morning papers.

As we sped back to Istanbul late on Sunday afternoon, I felt that living for a weekend within Muslim culture had something

Accidentally Istanbul

oddly familiar about it. Where I should have felt strange, I had felt comfortable, relaxed. Six months before if someone had told me I would be sharing *Iftar* with a Muslim family I wouldn't have believed it—and yet it felt normal, natural.

But it was Ted's comment that evening that tied my thoughts together.

'You know,' he said over a glass of wine, 'Seref reminds me of my Dad.'

'Really?'

'Dad was very conservative, you know. He spent his whole life working for the bank, doing what he thought was expected.'

So was that it? I wondered, extrapolating from his comment. *The warmth, the humour, the integrity, the conservatism, were familiar beasts simply clothed in different raiments. The core, the eternal flow of family life, was the same.*

19

Getting a visa

As I was trying to prepare a lesson, I overheard Ted on the phone to the University.

'Thank you, yes. I see—thank you,' I heard him saying, ever-polite.

But he was praying as he put down the phone. Well, that was my interpretation. He was saying 'Jesus Christ' and 'Almighty God' a lot, but there were other words that really had no place in a prayer.

'What did they say?' I asked innocently.

'They say the same f*^%*&^ thing every time I speak to them and every question I ask,' he said, with a reluctant grin. He looked as though he couldn't make up his mind whether to be angry or amused.

'*No problem, no problem*, they say,' he went on fuming. '*We will fix everything. Don't you worry.* I'm sure that mostly they're not even listening.'

'What *were* you asking?'

'All the things I've been asking just about every day: visas, work permits, taxation.'

In the weeks before our arrival in Istanbul, the University staff had made it sound as though *everything* could include the moon and the stars. There was absolutely nothing that Bahçeşehir University and its staff could not fix with a mere wave of a hand. Apartment, course times, visas, tax: *they will all be worked out in good time. Yes, yes—don't worry.* It was like a mantra.

Wanting to be a law-abiding citizen, Ted had been particularly concerned about a working visa. But after he started at the University, no one mentioned it. We were both acutely aware that our tourist visas would expire 90 days from our arrival. When Ted persisted, they smilingly prevaricated.

I also asked at the Berlitz School. The manager who had employed me sounded vague, even mystified.

'A work visa? That's for you to organise.'

One of the other teachers, overhearing, laughed as she drew me without much subtlety into a corner of the staff room. 'I actually applied for a working visa when I came here eight months ago.'

'And?' Now I was getting somewhere!

'And nothing. My mistake. I've never even had a reply. So I'm wiser now. Forget it. No one ever worries about it. You have a tax file number?'

Accidentally Istanbul

'Yes, they took me to the tax office on my first day to get that.'

'That will do you then, dearie,' she said, and hurried away to her class.

Another teacher took over. 'I've been here for five years now—and I'm still on a tourist visa.'

'So what do you do every three months when it runs out?'

'I go to Greece or Bulgaria or sometimes I go home to see the family in Dorset.'

To me, to 'going to Greece or Bulgaria' every three months sounded a splendid idea.

For the rest of Istanbul there were larger considerations than our visa worries. As autumn drew in and the days were often rainy and cold, we heard that finally, *finally*, the EU had given Turkey a date for accession talks. As Turks absorbed this news, further passionate debates began in every living room and tea-house. We joined in gladly, often as sponges rather than participants.

In spite of Ted's fuming, there eventually seemed no alternative but to have our tourist visas renewed. We set off with a plan as recommended by my helpful fellow teachers. We were to take a bus to the border of Bulgaria in the morning, cross and re-cross, and be back with a new three-month visa by the evening. I wasn't really looking forward to this. Hours sitting in a bus was not my idea of an exciting weekend. But maybe Bulgaria offered sightseeing possibilities.

With its 70 million people, Turkey had hundreds of coach

Accidentally Istanbul

services carrying thousands on overnight journeys to the most remote locations. However, these large coaches were not allowed into central Istanbul. Instead, you travelled by minibus to something called an *otogar* or bus station to pick up the cross-country coach.

The *otogar* was like a vast international airline terminal for coaches. A naturally deep valley had cleverly been used for parking, both for passengers and for the coaches not in service, with the terminal constructed over the top. On arrival we were shown upstairs to a very simple 'salon' spread with seats similar to an airline departure lounge. A glass wall looked out over a large village square with dozens of shopfronts. But in this particular square, busy with people hurrying in every direction, each shop window fronted a bus departure terminal.

We stared, amazed. There must have been 50 shopfronts, each an independent coach company. Spreading out behind these tiny terminals like a giant wheel were the hundreds of coaches destined for all corners of the country. The very size of the place was extraordinary. I was again reminded that my expectations were rarely accurate. Living in Turkey was like arriving through the looking-glass into a world where nothing was as anticipated—just like Alice.

How comfortable the coaches appeared as we boarded! There was plenty of leg-room and seductively comfortable reclining seats. They were also equipped with television screens for every passenger.

Accidentally Istanbul

We settled into our seats talking about how advanced Turkey's cross-country transport system was.

'I can't find my seatbelt,' grumbled Ted, his hand scrambling behind him.

'They must be here somewhere. I've found the slot, but I can't find the belt.'

But there were no seatbelts. The slots were there but the belts themselves had been removed. We chuckled at the contrast of comfort versus safety.

'Typical Turkish!' I said.

Ted was more explicit. 'I can't believe these idiots go to so much expense in providing super-luxurious coaches—and then remove the seatbelts. What are they thinking?'

He grumbled on, but we settled back to enjoy the ride, two-and-a-half hours to the town closest to the border with Bulgaria, Edirne. An attendant in a smart uniform brought plastic tea and coffee, Coca-Cola and cake.

'Just like Qantas,' Ted quipped.

'The cake is stale,' I said.

'Just like Qantas,' Ted grinned, looking out the window as we joined the eight-lane motorway.

We were looking forward to Edirne. Its history was like a fairy-tale. I had read that it was already in existence over 2000 years ago, home to an ancient tribe of Thracians. Then it became the city-state of Hadrian, named after himself by this most famous Roman Emperor. Later it was the eastern capital of the

Accidentally Istanbul

Greek Empire until Istanbul, then in the hands of the Greeks, was conquered.

Significant remnants of Edirne's heritage remained. Reading of its fountains, bath-houses, bridges, bazaars, proliferation of inns and antique markets, not to mention its tombs, theological schools, alms-houses and mosques, I looked forward to it.

We had also learned that the greatest work of art to be found in a mosque was in Edirne, Selimiye Cami (*cami*, pronounced *jarmi*, is such an elegant word compared with the surly-sounding 'mosque'.) Sultan Suleiman's greatest architect, the revered Koca Sinan, who built many mosques in Turkey, called this his masterpiece.

One of my students was a slim, ascetic young graduate doctor who worked at one of the large Istanbul hospitals. Cem (pronounced Jem) was quiet in class, but diligent. He had told me he was in love with a girl from Edirne and would be visiting her while we intended to be there.

'Maybe we meet in afternoon,' he had suggested very shyly (Turks are *very* bad at articles). 'We show you special things of Edirne, yes? Nice.'

'Why, that would be excellent,' I replied with frank enthusiasm. 'We *will* meet in *the* afternoon,' added the schoolteacher.

'*Evet, evet* (Yes, yes),' he smiled, 'we *will* meet in *the* afternoon.'

'Edirne is not ordinary town,' he added mysteriously. 'Many, many strange thing in Edirne.' He would not be drawn further, but his normally serious young face lit up with smiles.

Accidentally Istanbul

'You see,' he said. 'I show you.'

On arrival in Edirne's *otogar*, we took a *dolmus* (minibus) to Kapıkule, or Tower Door, the gateway to Bulgaria. The border looked like Checkpoint Charlie, all concrete, wire fences and dismal buildings, and it didn't fill me with optimism, particularly as, at the time this happened, I was still sporting a crutch from my fall down the steps in the restaurant. No-man's land seemed to stretch for miles, not simply 500 metres.

The Turkish officer at the first checkpoint smiled with grandfatherly warmth under his hairy moustache and luxuriant hair, stared at my wooden crutch. He started making large hand-gestures at my crutch and the road, shrugging his shoulders, and shaking his head.

We were astonished when he stopped the next car, and after a few words of hurried Turkish, hustled us with big swooping arm movements into the back seat. I had images of being kidnapped by the Turkish or Bulgarian underworld. I could already see the headlines in Australia: *Australian couple disappear without trace in Eastern Europe.*

The driver, so suddenly press-ganged into transporting total strangers across the border, had a mild face and a pot-belly bulging against the steering wheel. He did not seem much like a kidnapper. He didn't speak English, so while we waited in seemingly interminable queues to cross the barren concrete wasteland, we all smiled at each other encouragingly, and I tried in my simple Turkish to make what passed for conversation.

Accidentally Istanbul

On the Bulgarian side, the officers were serious, efficient and authoritarian. It was obviously not a joking matter to want to enter their country. Ted and I maintained suitably serious faces to suit their demeanour while they eyed us with something verging on distaste.

With many farewells and thanks to our Good Samaritan, we were let off at a brick-built restaurant several metres past the checkpoint. Our inadvertent chauffeur accelerated away, with a friendly, if hesitant, smile.

We ate a bleak lunch on a concrete verandah. The service was sober and reluctant. Smiles, to which we had become so accustomed in Istanbul, were absent.

When we began our walk back through the border, we were looking forward to returning to the friendliness of the Turks. One of their officers, who had waved us past to the Bulgarian checkpoint just half an hour before, was still on duty. When he saw us approaching, he recognised us immediately, started to smile, but then frowned.

We stopped, uncertain. I thought *Oh no no no, we're in trouble now. He's going to give us a hard time because we're returning so quickly.* There was a moment when I wanted to turn back into Bulgaria and I started to feel for Ted's hand to drag him with me. *This was a mistake. We should have stayed longer ... maybe overnight ...*

But then the officer's face became wreathed in even bigger smiles. '*Ah! formalité, formalité!*' he said, beckoning us through.

Accidentally Istanbul

Ted smiled back. 'Yes, formality, formality,' he repeated, and the officer then did the most extraordinary thing. He took a couple of steps towards us and shook our hands, first Ted's, then mine. We were taken aback, but tried not to show it, smiling and nodding.

'What was all that about?' I muttered as soon as we moved on.

'Hanged if I know,' said Ted. 'Maybe he's pleased we want to go back to Turkey.'

How long was it going to take us to work out what these people were thinking?

The rest of the afternoon we were free to explore Edirne. We phoned my student Cem to arrange our meeting, then caught the *dolmuş*.

We had agreed to meet at the gate of the Selimiye Cami. We were both awed by the enormous building which rose in cream layers, then arches and towers like cake decorations, with lustrous chocolate lips dividing them. The highest layer was charcoal, all tall pillars and shining glass and garlanded with four mighty minarets swooping to the sky. Its presence dominated everything on earth, tempting as the sun.

Meltem, Cem's fiancée, was a long-legged girl with a heavy load of sleek dark hair which waved behind her when she moved, like one of those slow-motion hair commercials. She had warm brown eyes which expressed more than her words and I took to her immediately. She seemed shy, but spoke English much better than Cem. We chatted for a while, learning a little

Accidentally Istanbul

about their lives, their studies and their marriage plans. Then it was time to enter the mosque and I noticed that Meltem had a neckscarf ready (as I did) to draw over her head for respectful entry. I was reminded of my early childhood, when ladies who didn't wear a hat wore a scarf to enter a church. *There are some things about these two religions which are so similar*, the thought came unbidden.

The grounds were deserted, pigeons the only inhabitants, cooing and chirping in the bleak white sky of the chilly autumn afternoon. There had been rain and the long stone paths were puddled and shining. A slim young woman in a headscarf and skin-tight black jeans was sweeping the leaves from the pathways ever so slowly, with a broom made of twigs, like a witch's broom. She watched us, frankly staring, never ceasing her sweeping. I wondered fleetingly what she thought of the hordes of Westerners (*yabancı*) who trailed through her domain with their strange clothes and loud voices.

As we approached the door where we were to remove our shoes, there were two old women, also headscarfed and wearing voluminous flowered dresses, selling plastic bags in which to place our shoes.

Ted pulled out two single million-*lira* coins from his pocket and gave me one. I handed this to the woman and she nodded, giving me a used plastic bag that I would get free in the supermarket. Ted, slightly behind me, offered the same, but she held up two fingers.

Accidentally Istanbul

'No, never,' said the suddenly affronted Ted, and began to walk rapidly past. The woman changed her mind quickly and accepted the coin.

'You didn't have to pay them at all,' remarked Cem as we were taking off our shoes in the foyer.

'I know,' I said, 'but our friends in Istanbul have explained that it gives them an income.'

'And it's better than simply begging,' explained Ted.

'Of course you're right!' Cem seemed delighted at this small lesson we had learned.

Inside I tiptoed, not wanting to break the silence. Large circles of lights strung on wires hung just above us in concentric circles. The ceiling rose majestically, every inch covered in a complexity of patterns and colours, with vast rhythmic archways flying high into the grey light overhead. I felt a kind of dizziness at my smallness in this awesome towering womb.

In a far corner just one man prayed, oblivious to us. I felt like an intruder, as I would have in a church where someone was praying.

We admired, silently, and then slipped out just as quietly.

'Now we take you to Alipaşa Pazar,' said Cem with some authority. 'It is biggest in city and you find amazing things there.'

We set off through the busy streets. The almost-bare trees formed delicate silhouettes against the white sky as they bent over the hubbub of the pavements. From the end of each

Accidentally Istanbul

street we could see a misty vision of towers and domes, the old keeping watch over the new, with the new represented by a chaotic tangle of electric wires stretching along and across all the streets, marring the otherwise graceful scene.

Edirne was all small shops and intimate arcades, devoid of modern shopping malls. The shoppers were fresh-faced from the cold. Juices were being sold from rough wooden tables on the footpath, one million *lira* ($1) per glass. Occasionally, a tea-seller hurried by, three or four small Turkish glasses of tea balanced daintily on the tray on the palm of his outstretched hand. Cem said that many tradespeople placed regular orders, and tea-sellers made their living solely from tea sales.

At my mention of the tea-sellers, the typically instant Turkish response came from our shy host.

'Will you like tea now?'

'No thank you—later. I was just interested.'

Elaborate street stalls, painted carefully in yellows and reds, were often on wheels that looked suspiciously as though they came from someone's bicycle. Wide trays held lusciously-coloured vegetables, the brightest purple, red and orange contrasting with the dark rich green of leafy sprays. As I passed I wondered if I was dreaming when I smelled the pungent soil in which they were grown. Cem confirmed the food was home-grown so the smell of soil was normal.

One street seller offered only enormous leeks; another sold only cabbages. They stood, wrapped warmly in parkas, scarves

Accidentally Istanbul

and beanies, one hand often shoved deep into a pocket while the other held the inevitable cigarette. Shop owners leant in their doorways dressed in traditional garb: all-white for bakers and striped aprons for butchers, and all had a smile for passers-by. I was again reminded of my childhood picture books where bakers and butchers were dressed like this.

A knife-sharpener stood on a corner concentrating hard on his sharpening contraption, which looked like a weirdly-shaped foot-operated sewing machine. A small queue of people waited patiently, knives in hands.

We saw many mothers with tiny children, some in headscarves and drab straight coats, others with long hair blowing in the wind and tight jeans. I could have spent all day just looking. As we wandered and watched, I thought of what I had read. These cobbled streets had been trodden for so many thousands of years. Imagination took over. I could easily see the ghosts of Greeks and Romans in tunics and togas, walking here just where we were among the fountains and monuments. Opulently-dressed sultans passed by in their carriages, too, horses prancing, right in front of me.

'What are you doing? Are you coming?' Ted's voice, from far ahead, was tinged with exasperation. Cem and Meltem were looking back curiously.

'Yes yes—I'm coming.'

We had finally reached Edirne's biggest covered bazaar, also designed by the great Sinan. We were glad to escape into its

Accidentally Istanbul

warmth and darkness. It was lit by the lights of the shops and high windows in the ancient arched ceiling. In the long alcove we could see everything from knitting wool to running shoes and antique clocks for sale.

While Cem was pointing out all the wonderful goods: treasures made from onyx, vases and egg-cups and tall statues, soft leather jackets, gloves, curious hand-made goods of many designs and fabrics, Ted said: 'Look!'

He was gazing up towards the roof, marvelling. High arches and pillars swept the eye upwards, their lines making music in the air, remote from the earthly clamour of the market-trading below. I smiled. Ted was ever the architect, hardly noticing the vibrant human scene around us, but spellbound by the sweet lines and grand statements of the walls and ceiling above us.

Cem had 'something special' to show us. Full of expectations, we were led to a shop which seemed to sell only plastic fruit. Cem and Meltem stood back and waited for our reaction. There was a high sugary confusion of aromas coming from the fruit.

'Nice perfume,' I said. And 'I've never seen so many different types of plastic fruit.'

'No, no—you don't understand.' Cem was frowning. 'These are carved soap, not plastic. They've been a specialty of Edirne for hundreds of years.'

I stepped forward, now more interested. Lemons and oranges, grapes and apples, strawberries and watermelon were so finely wrought it was hard to believe they were hand-made here in

Accidentally Istanbul

Edirne. They looked as though they had been bulk-produced in some Chinese factory.

Meltem, with her better grasp of English, explained: 'As you know, this was the capital of the Ottoman Empire for many years, and the daughters and concubines of the sultans and the other court ladies competed for these sweet-smelling fruit soaps. They collected them for their trousseaux, so every other young girl wanted them too. That's how the tradition began. Now Edirne soaps are famous all over the world.'

I smiled inwardly, wondering how many Americans or Australians or Nigerians would know about Edirne soaps. But we collected enough to fill a good fruit bowl.

Outside again, we passed down a street of old wooden Ottoman houses, so elegant in their construction, the upper level overhanging the ground floor. Cem stopped in the middle of the street. 'So now the best moment of the day.'

The building in front of us was in the Ottoman style, but the shop was painted daisy yellow with burgundy windows.

'This is original liver restaurant,' said Cem. 'It's called *Niyazi Usta* and serves best liver in all Turkey.'

Liver was hardly my favourite meal as a child. As soon as I was old enough I would do anything to avoid being at home if liver was being served. *No*, I thought immediately, *definitely not liver*.

Cem and Meltem had been so kind, but I had to be honest. 'I don't actually like liver very much. Maybe you three can eat, and I'll just watch.'

'But this is nothing like any other liver. *Nothing* tastes as good as this liver.'

Eating liver was obviously to be my punishment for coming to Edirne. We trooped in out of the cold and were seated at the warmth of a corner table.

Maybe they won't notice if I just eat a little ...

In a blur of incomprehensible Turkish our meal was ordered, with the inevitable tiny glasses of tea arriving first without our asking.

'This restaurant is here more than 30 years, owned by same family,' began Cem. We chatted more about Edirne and its fabulous history. I was thinking: *But I can't smell liver. You can always smell liver.*

When it arrived it resembled a plate of potato crisps. Very finely-sliced liver had been stir-fried. Plucking up courage, I took a piece. The taste was fresh, light and moreish. I ate the lot.

Cem suddenly called out across the restaurant to a handsome middle-aged man, who then hurried away.

'That's Niyazi Bey himself here today,' Cem explained excitedly. I'm very happy. He's going to show us how liver is chopped.'

It was as though a symphony concert were about to begin or a Shakespearean play. The pace of the restaurant immediately quickened. Waiters smartly removed our plates and cleaned our table, even replacing the tablecloth. Two chefs ran out from

Accidentally Istanbul

behind the scenes, complete with their white hats and aprons. Niyazi Bey himself stood a little apart, chatting, hardly noticing what was happening.

The chefs carried a cutting board between them with great ceremony. Then an underling arrived and placed on the board, horror of horrors, a dark red slab of raw calf's liver dripping with blood. I felt my stomach turn. Then everyone stood back for the *usta* (maestro) to begin.

His knife had to be unbelievably sharp. The meat was fresh and unfrozen, yet he cut the glistening and trembling slab into tiny slivers so fine you could see through them as he flamboyantly raised them to the light. In among the good red liver there were minuscule strings of fat—or was it sinew?—which he removed quickly and expertly, placing them in a small pile at the edge of the cutting board. He wielded the knife with a precision and elegance that was a pleasure to watch.

The other diners were also fascinated, and the chefs and waiters stood by respectfully. Niyazi *Usta* (Niyazi the Master) did not speak a word of English, but there was no question that he understood our fascination with this amazing culinary demonstration. It was lucky that Cem and Meltem could fully express our appreciation. We were grateful for this new small insight into Turkish life.

'I'm glad we're here on a tourist visa,' said Ted back in Istanbul that evening. 'Think what fun we're going to have every three months!'

Accidentally Istanbul

'*Every* three months? This one will last until the end of the semester—so we won't need another,' I said quickly.

'You're right,' said Ted, equally fast. 'But we might keep sailing for a while along the Turkish coastline, so we may still need to renew it.'

'Of course, yes. Great.'

With this happy prospect I went to bed with spiralling thoughts of sailing into the spring and then summer along the coastline of Turkey, and maybe on to Greece. As I drifted off to sleep, my waking dreams were of the wind in my hair and sunshine sparkling on the water.

20

Falling under the spell

I eventually began to take our new lifestyle for granted: teaching English and loving my students; getting to know my new group of English-speaking friends; and exploring this great city.

My vision seemed to clear. The cats in the alleys no longer offended me. Rather I was often stopped in my tracks by the sights around me, overcome by a sudden warmth, an inexplicable gladness making me draw breath and sigh.

I was falling in love. Not with a man, but with a city. I tried to work out why. *Why do I love thee?* I thought, in a variation of Elizabeth Browning's meaning. *Let me count the ways.*

It was not the beauty of Istanbul—though that was spellbinding—or the mist that stole around the steeples in the crisp early-morning air or the skyline of cupolas and domes and minarets against a red sunset, or the great ships that march like

Accidentally Istanbul

armies up the Bosphorus.

It was not the musky smell of spices in the bazaar, the raucous shouting of fish vendors, the anarchy of busy ferries on the Golden Horn, the thousands of hustling fishermen on every foreshore or the chaos of new buildings jammed against ancient grey stone walls. Nor was it the clouds of yellow leaves blowing over the wet streets, or the spindly trees of autumn with their first brushing of snow. It was not even the elegant beauty of the old palaces or the unexpected tiny treasure shops found in winding back streets. No—it was none of these things, although all would beguile a casual visitor.

I realised, as my bus trundled along through choked traffic in the mornings, that it was instead a million small, subtle things. I appreciated the helpful young man patiently walking an elderly person across the street, holding one hand up to halt the traffic, the other at the ready to support her, then smiling a gentle farewell and striding off. I loved the kind, proud smile on the face of an elderly man basking on the pavement in a patch of winter sunshine.

Memories crowded my mind: the cashier in a busy restaurant who left the till open to walk clear across the room at the call of a customer; the taxi driver who returned me the 10 million *lira* note that I had mistaken for a one million (not that there weren't scallywag taxi-drivers too); the bazaar vendor who always threw in a tomato with your beans, or put an apple in with the spinach, with a grin and a conspiratorial nod; the bright

Accidentally Istanbul

eyed enthusiasm of the young people swapping stories on the bus, scarves flying, mouths chattering, friends hugging, diving headlong into their future. Their shiny cheeks and big smiles seemed to tell a story. Was it a story about belief in a future where Turkey and their world could only get better?

Such an old civilisation. Such a new world.

21

Guests

Ted and I were travelling in a local *dolmus*, a 'go-when-it's-full' scheduled-route minivan. Where there were no regular bus services, the *dolmus* was the cheap Turkish alternative. Thousands of entrepreneurial drivers made a living this way. Sometimes there were identifiable stops but more often one just needed to catch the driver's eye.

We scrambled on to the minivan along with young men in jeans who leapt in and old ladies in headscarves who bent stiffly as they clambered up awkwardly. The driver paid little attention. No one seemed to be paying a fare. We found ourselves seats towards the back.

More people kept getting on even when all seats were taken. Some sat on plastic footstools, some on the floor. Then everyone rearranged their seating so that men and women (unless in a

Accidentally Istanbul

family) didn't sit together. One of the passengers slid the door shut with a bang, and the minivan moved off.

People were passing their fares forward hand-to-hand to the driver, who sent the change and tickets back by the same method, while driving through heavy traffic. The assumption of total honesty was impressive. It led to chaos, however, with people getting on and off and, as they alighted, throwing their fares back to other passengers to hand forward.

No one looked as if they spoke English so I could ask about the fare. After watching for a few minutes I deduced that it was 750,000 *lira* (roughly 75 cents) and passed forward two million-*lira* coins. Back came change of one million *lira* and 250,000 *kuruş*, with one ticket. So the fare was right—but the driver had only taken money for one person.

I waited for a quiet traffic moment, then swung forward to a seat closer to the front, proffering 750,000 *lira* to another passenger to pass forward.

After some incomprehensible muttering with the driver, the passenger held up one finger and said: '*Hayir, Bir million lira* (No, one million *lira*).'

I was astonished. Was he charging us an inflated price?

'No,' I said. 'Only 750,000 *lira*!' But of course he didn't understand me.

'One million *lira*!' he repeated, this time in English, surprising me. Was there one price for the locals and another for tourists? I started to feel angry, but looked at him in puzzlement, shaking my head and shrugging my shoulders. This was not fair—and I was reluctant to let it pass.

Another passenger then joined in, talking to me rapidly in Turkish. I had no idea what he was saying. I tried again.

'One ticket, 750,000 *lira*?' I asked.

This caused an outburst from all sides. Everyone was talking at once but I had no idea what they were saying. They were talking to me, to one another, to the bus driver and to my intermediary, all at once. It was deafening.

The driver was turning round to shout at some of the passengers. 'No! No!' I said, giggling nervously. 'You drive!' waving his attention back to the road. Some of the other passengers understood my hand gestures and laughed with me. The driver, however, just went on twisting in his seat in intense conversation with the others.

I was feeling not only embarrassed at the growing commotion, but quite confused. Ted was cowering in his seat staring out the window, trying to pretend he wasn't with me.

Finally I heard through the hubbub a voice in English towards the back of the minivan. 'You're right,' she called. 'The fare is 75,000 *lira*. So you have to pay one million five hundred thousand *lira* for the two of you.'

This summing-up, which she repeated to the crowd in Turkish, caused even more commotion. They began arguing with her as well. I couldn't make her hear me above the noise, so I lurched back along the aisle and plomped into an adjacent empty seat.

Accidentally Istanbul

'I don't actually care about the money, but I've already paid for one ticket at 750,000 *lira*,' I explained. 'So now I only have to pay for one extra. But the driver is asking for one million.'

'Oh, I see,' she said kindly, and launched into an explanation to the whole bus. The driver now seemed incidental to the affair—which was good, since it meant he could concentrate on the road. After some shouting back and forth, my new friend's face lit up with understanding.

'Ah, now I see,' she said happily, 'The driver is only charging you 500,000 *lira* each because you are guests in our country. He was asking you for one million *lira* for two, not one. So I've explained you've already paid for one and now only have to pay 500,000 more.'

This seemed to clinch it. Everyone gradually settled down, smiles all round, and people returning to their own conversations.

When we alighted it was among a laughing cacophony of shouted farewells, with much waving and encouraging pats on the shoulder. We waved back and grinned like actors taking applause.

'More hospitality like that,' I muttered to Ted between gritted teeth as we walked away, 'and I'll soon be a nervous wreck.'

But he was not listening. He was smiling at some obviously funny private joke. Finally he said: 'That was a bad deal you made there.'

'Why? What do you mean?'

'We paid 500,000 *lira* for one of us, but 750,000 *lira* for

Accidentally Istanbul

the other, when he was charging us only 500,000 *lira*. So you've overpaid by 250,000 *lira*. Shouldn't you have asked for a refund?'

It's best to ignore Ted sometimes.

We walked on a few paces and then I stopped.

'What's the matter?' he asked, turning back.

'I'm just taking it in,' I said. 'The driver reduced our fare because we are *guests in Turkey*.'

I was still thinking about this for days afterwards, trying to imagine a similar situation in the United States or Australia or in fact anywhere I had lived. Of course, I couldn't. A tourist, a foreigner, is always fair game for overcharging, not the recipient of discounts.

Further, the driver of a *dolmus* is running his own business so he took the money out of his own pocket—and I wouldn't even have *known* if I hadn't noticed the fares others were paying. I had great difficulty getting inside the mind of such a person. He was obviously not rich and worked hard for a living—yet he took it upon himself to reduce our fare.

I still had so much to learn about this country …

22

Rogues, thieves and drivers

Experiences like ours in the minivan might suggest everyone in Turkey was generous and welcoming. Not so. We were warned fairly early of the slippery ways of the rogue Istanbul taxi driver.

Gül's university-student son Ali, who spoke excellent English, took great delight in explaining all the ways that a thieving driver could outwit an innocent client. '"Daytime rate",' he informed us, 'shows on the meter as *gündüz*, flashing on and off with the fare. But a rogue driver may turn it to the night rate. So if you don't see *gündüz*, you should point to the meter and say *problem*.' He pronounced this the French way. 'Or with very new taxis, maybe it just says: "1" for day rate and "2"' for night rate. You must always check.'

The other ruse was to tell you that the normal route was 'blocked with traffic' so that you must now take another, longer

Accidentally Istanbul

one. The word they used was *kalabalık*, meaning crowded. If we heard this word in a driver's conversation, we should be very suspicious. A friend of his visiting from Eskisehir had been driven to Asia and back again, taking 45 minutes instead of ten.

Mostly such behaviour happens in tourist areas. I, by contrast, had drivers retrieve my wallet from the back seat where I had left it, and drivers who reminded me that the note I had just given gave them was a 50, not a ten. Broadly I found they were an honest bunch of god-fearing—or should I say Allah-fearing?—citizens.

We did, however, uncover a nasty scam from one unlucky experience. We discovered after the event that an unscrupulous taxi driver can even 'fix' his meter so that it runs at four times the normal speed. One day we took a taxi home together from the University, a trip that usually cost around 12 million *lira* (about $12). As we pulled up on our street, it read 42 million *lira*. Aghast, we leapt out of the taxi and Ted began arguing, completely unabashed by the fact that the driver could not understand a word. It was just as well, because had he been a religious man he would have been offended. Ted was also questioning his intelligence and sanity and saying quite terrible things about his mother.

Undeterred, the driver also kept up a loud stream of Turkish, with the words *kırk-iki million lira* (42 million *lira*) prominent. I giggled in the background while they argued, one in English, the other in Turkish, with only the word *lira* in common.

Accidentally Istanbul

It was when Ted turned round and said: 'Nance, call the police!' that I started to get worried, mostly because I doubted policemen would speak English. In any case, I didn't know their phone number.

'Right,' I said gamely, taking out my cellphone.

Then two things happened. I've mentioned that our block of apartments was near a university. First we were approached by an ambling group of young people who were obviously students, shoulder bags swinging, long, dark hair shining down the backs of both boys and girls.

'What is the problem?' asked one of the young men, while the rest of the group, boys and girls together, stopped to listen.

Ted explained.

Instantly one young man, laughing and sighing and running his fingers through his hair like a comb, stepped in front of Ted and took over the conversation with the driver in rapid-fire Turkish. The others joined in too, and they all seemed to be talking to the poor man at once, pinning him against his car door.

'How much do you think you should pay?' one turned to ask.

'It normally costs about 12 million *lira*.'

'Give me that then.'

Ted obediently handed over the exact amount.

Simultaneously with this our *kapıcı*, the doorman from our building, appeared beside me. He had obviously heard the shouts and general ruckus going on and crossed the street to join us.

He rattled off something in Turkish and then, with an urgent

Accidentally Istanbul

smile, grabbed Ted by the sleeve and marched us away across the street to our block. We left the students still in hot debate with the now chastened and humbled driver, still flattened against his taxi. Some of them waved and nodded approvingly to our *kapıcı* as we were hauled across the street, shocked and laughing and calling *thank you* back over our shoulders.

We finally learned what to look for in order to recognise an honest driver. All taxis in Istanbul are yellow, but on some, in the middle of the front door appears the name of the car's base. Other drivers are freelance and answer to no one. From then on, when possible, we chose a base-identified taxi. We found their drivers honest and helpful.

Travelling by taxi, which I did frequently to teach corporate executives to speak colloquial English in their boardrooms, offered one of the best opportunities to practise my fault-filled Turkish. Turkish drivers are frequently fond of chatting, but sometimes it takes an ice-breaker, since many seemed shy about speaking with a Western woman.

The greatest ice-breaker of all was to ask where someone lived and if he had children. This would immediately bring a glad response. Typically, the driver's eyes would light up with love as he talked about his family, his children and grandchildren. He would then ask about mine. I might be a strangely tall and blonde Westerner from a distant country, but I was also, just like Turkish women, a mother and a wife and we could both easily discuss our children.

Accidentally Istanbul

These conversations did much to allay my feeling of foreignness, the fact that we could communicate on some universal level that ignored culture, politics and religion, all the things that divide us. The love of family and belonging was something we could genuinely share. These conversations left me lighthearted, buzzing with feelings of connection. They were a small addition to my day that kept me smiling into the evening.

23

Dogs that own themselves

I came to love trying out my infantile Turkish, sometimes with hilarious results, but often thwarted by the fact that most Turks with a modicum of English wanted to practise that too.

One day Ted and I were in a busy central cafe drinking Turkish tea. I had quickly become addicted both to the tea and to watching the faces in the crowd. This day a large dog slept nearby sprawled across the pavement. He was larger than a labrador, cream in colour with a dark head and sad, drooping eyes. He slept with one eye open but people wanting to pass were forced to step around or over him.

Amused, I asked the waiter in Turkish: 'Who owns him?'

While Ted was the more charismatic, the one to whom people always immediately warmed, in company with strangers I always started the conversations. Ted remained stoically monolingual.

Accidentally Istanbul

'Us', grinned the waiter in English, with an expansive gesture that seemed to take in the whole world.

'You mean he belongs to the restaurant?' I reverted to English.

He was laughing as he gathered dirty plates. 'No, no—he doesn't belong to anyone except himself.'

This seemed pretty cold-hearted. 'Is there no dog pound in Turkey that would pick him up and take care of him?'

The waiter, a moustachioed man with broad shoulders and an even broader stomach, sighed audibly. He came over to our table.

As he leaned over me, his voice was kindly. 'I know. I lived in Germany for a while. There if someone doesn't claim a dog, he is sent to the pound and probably that's the end of his life. I will come back ...' He sped away, swaying between tables, managing a mountain of plates with awe-inspiring dexterity.

Soon he was back, wiping his hands on a towel. He placed both of them squarely on the back of the vacant seat at our table. 'We have always believed that dogs belong to themselves, not to us. So we love them and feed them—but we don't own them.'

'I see,' I said. 'But he's very tame.' I was thinking of the wild dogs of the desert hills of Egypt, where the locals shoot them if they can.

He laughed at this, moving away again, gathering more plates, calling over his shoulder as he went: 'He knows everyone loves him, that dog.'

Accidentally Istanbul

Then he was back again. 'It's true the *Sahipsiz Hayvanları Koruma Derneği* [he said this so fast I could hardly understand] does sometimes pick them up. But they only give them their vaccinations and put them back where they found them.'

He marched away, balancing plates and cups and leftovers and knives and forks above the crowd, leaving us to speculate (correctly, as it turned out) that he must be talking about the Turkish RSPCA.

As diners started to drift away, he came back to our table yet again. I had obviously hit on a subject dear to his heart. 'This dog is not an ordinary dog,' he said, one hand on fat hip, gazing affectionately at the huge creature. 'He's not tame. He is merely calm, like a king.'

Regal was not a word I would have used, but the dog was certainly self-contained, with placid eyes.

The waiter went on. 'Do you know about the Kangal? It's Turkey's own dog breed—but nothing like any dog you've ever seen.'

With that he sat down at our table in an easy, familiar way and one of the other waiters, watching, brought him a cup of coffee. *Was this his restaurant?*

He explained that the Kangal is an age-old breed of sheep dog with its roots going back into pre-history. It lives with its flock on the mountainside and protects them from wolves or other attack. When the sheep are frightened, they run *to* the Kangal, never away from it.

Accidentally Istanbul

This protective instinct is not just for sheep. Once a Kangal dog identifies its family, animal or human, it will protect it with uncommon loyalty. It is extremely gentle and seems to understand that the smallest humans or animals need the most protection, so it is wonderful for a household with tiny children and babies.

'Of course, this dog is quite small for a Kangal—so maybe he is not *all* Kangal.'

I stared at the huge dog. 'Small?'

'Most Kangals are much larger—maybe *this* high at the shoulder.' His hand was higher than the table. He smiled. 'This dog knows his special heritage.'

Ted and I thanked the informative waiter and left, much the richer. This was quite a new way of thinking about pets. The words rang over and over in my mind: *he belongs to himself.*

While I gleaned insights through such chance meetings, I gained different perspectives from more complex discussions with my new friends in the book club.

They were able to explain the culture and many of the customs of Turkey, from both positive and negative perspectives. In English we have polite phrases: *Please, Thank you, Excuse me.* But there are surprisingly few, not even a shared English expression for the French *Bon appétit.*

There are many more in Turkish. I found myself entranced. *Geçmiş olsun* I had already learned was the polite response for someone suffering illness or bad luck: it means 'May it pass

Accidentally Istanbul

quickly.' Welcome, *Hoş Geldiniz,* has a rejoinder, *Hoş Bulduk,* which means something like 'I'm glad to be here.' The Turkish version of *Bon appétit, Afiyet olsun,* has a rejoinder, *Elene salık.* This is said to the cook and means 'health to your hands'.

There are many others. And it was not only the language that fascinated me. These protocols of politeness and gentility penetrated to the core of the community. I felt strangely humbled, having always thought the English were masters of courtesy and etiquette.

There were other secrets to learn. No people lived on the street and we saw no beggars, except the occasional Romani (gypsy). But there was no safety net either—no dole and no universal aged pension as we know it. I couldn't reconcile these two facts. My new friends took it for granted that the family, the street, the village or the apartment block would look after old or ill people. As for the dole, if you could not find a job, you were expected to earn a living as best you could, often by selling something on the street. *So that's why there are so many street sellers.* These were considered honourable by their families, unlike our ingrained predilection to look down on such people.

I spent several days remembering how I had brushed past these people with their displays of socks and wallets and jewellery and scarves. Guilt plagued me as I thought of my past behaviour. *What did you want, Nancy, to have them all on the dole?* I didn't know; I didn't know. *You have always had so little respect for those who easily take the dole, without effort,* I chastised

Accidentally Istanbul

myself. I didn't know; I didn't know.

My respect for these people rose as high as my own self-image slumped. I also remembered the kindnesses I saw every day on the street. Why, these people looked after each other like family, whether they knew one another or not. The caring was genuine, just as Gül's caring made me feel like part of her family. It was as much part of her nature as her ready smiles and the daily biscuits she baked. She knew no other way of being.

I began to walk around my adopted city with new understanding and a new readiness to emulate and return the enveloping warmth that I was only now ready to accept. I enjoyed each day with no concept of the coming tumultuous events that would completely change my ideas about the country.

One aspect of Turkish culture appealed to my wild side—or was it the larrikin nature of my Australian background? *There must be a little Ned Kelly in all Australians*, I suggested to myself, conscious that I had not a trace of Irish blood.

Harking back to a nomadic past, Turkish tradition says: 'If one starts building after dusk and moves into a completed house before dawn the next day without having been noticed by the authorities, it cannot be just torn down by police, who must merely start legal action. Effectively, the house becomes yours.' This meant that thousands of Turkish people from eastern Anatolia had travelled to Istanbul to find work, claiming homes as their right. The houses are called *gece kondu* (pronounced *gedgee kondu*), which means 'night landing'. We found any

Accidentally Istanbul

empty public land, usually steep hillsides or the edges of railway lines, covered with *gece kondu* houses, flimsy shacks built of a million different materials.

What I loved most was that these people then secretly connected themselves to the power and water of adjoining mansions. Sometimes tax-paying law-abiding citizens would be paying the electricity bills and supplying the water of the *gece kondu* for years without realising. Such rascally ingenuity was captivating.

24

Feasts and festivals

Another four-day festival approached which did not involve fasting. Quite the opposite! Kurban Bayramı, the Feast of the Sacrifice, is a religious festival, but it is celebrated, like Christmas at home, whether one is religious or not. We were reminded that in Turkey, just like Australia, everyone loves a holiday, whatever the reason.

The origin is fascinating. It is based on the familiar story from the Bible where Abraham, to show his love for God, was willing to sacrifice his own son.

In the Bible story God intervened and allowed a sheep to be sacrificed instead and this festival celebrates the story with the slaughter of a sheep. When the population was not so dense I imagine it would have been one of those treasured rituals, just as in days gone by my grandfather killed a turkey for Christmas.

Accidentally Istanbul

However, in densely-populated Istanbul, killing a sheep at home is now considered a ghastly business, especially when done by accountants and lawyers and fishermen who don't know the first thing about how to do it cleanly and professionally. This means that the Feast of the Sacrifice has gained a less-than-savoury reputation among foreigners living in the city.

I was keen to observe this ritual killing at least once. But my English-speaking friends were aghast. 'You don't want to see that. They're trying to stop it.'

Osman delicately explained that ritual killing was not condoned among educated people. Over a glass of wine one evening, he told me: 'You can see this done by very conservative [I heard 'old-fashioned'] people. It's also done quite a lot in the countryside, but here in Istanbul the supermarkets will do it for you.'

'The supermarkets? How?'

He explained the tradition that one-third of the beast was for the family, another third shared with the extended family or people less well-off, and the final third was given to charity.

'The supermarket arranges it all with their butchers. You pay for three times what you receive, and the rest is distributed for you. It's much simpler that way.'

I still wanted to see it taking place at least once. Osman told me that sometimes a slaughter went wrong and a half-dead sheep might escape and run down the street. I could still remember Grandpa, a neat hand at killing chooks, occasionally getting it wrong so that a rooster would be flying all over our back yard with its head still dangling by a string of flesh.

Osman continued: 'To concentrate on the sacrifice itself is wrong for Kurban Bayramı. It's a time to get all the family together, and to visit others.'

He explained that the first day is for visiting parents and grandparents, who know to stay home. The second day is for visiting aunts and great-uncles, older cousins and maybe neighbours who are like family. The third day is for visiting your peers, your friends. So the celebration is a happy time of closeness including, for religious families, closeness to God, for whom Abraham set such a fine example by being willing to sacrifice his son.

Just as for Ramazan, there was a mass exodus from Istanbul. The traffic was crazy, with many freeway accidents and deaths. Many Istanbul-born people still do not identify it as their 'home' and return to the place of their grandparents and forebears to celebrate these rich traditions.

When the day came, no one, Turkish or foreigner, would admit that they knew where I could see a sacrifice. So we lunched with friends. The closest I came to seeing blood was a couple of street dogs dragging some large, fresh, bloody bones across the road on our way home. What an opportunity missed!

The next celebration was that of the death of Ataturk, Father of the Turks. As 10 November, the day in 1938 that Ataturk died at 9.05am approached, Istanbul became swathed with monstrous flags: hanging down most multi-storied buildings,

Accidentally Istanbul

on ferries and fishing boats, out of house windows or waved by children in the streets. To an Australian it seemed so *extreme*.

On the morning itself we were enjoying a late, lazy breakfast, since neither of us had early classes. Suddenly we heard the wailing of sirens.

'Listen! It's a fire!' I jumped up, knocking my tea flying across the glass table-top.

'Nance!' shouted Ted, not worried about the fire, but very worried that I had wet his toast and Vegemite. I couldn't see anything from the window but that all the traffic had come to a standstill.

'Maybe it's an earthquake. We should get outside.' But no one was running outside and the people in the front garden were standing still.

'It's strange,' I said. 'The traffic isn't moving on any of the streets. Even the cars over there with a green light signalling are not moving.'

Then I noticed a practice basketball match on the playing field over the road had halted, with the ball still rolling but the players standing stock-still. People on the footpaths were also quite still. It was as if the world had frozen over.

Puzzled, I turned to Ted who was still seated at the breakfast table, mopping up my tea with napkins. Now he glanced at me sideways, an amused smile on his face. 'Ataturk,' he said. 'It must be for Ataturk. Look—it's just after 9.05am.'

I looked at my watch: 9.06am.

Accidentally Istanbul

The breakfast table now returned to some semblance of order, Ted came over to the window to watch the spectacle with me. For two minutes the siren sounded, as the entire city of Istanbul halted to remember their great leader. As we stood I remembered how he had leap-frogged Turkey into a modern world. Inspired by liberal French writers, his actions were dramatic and fast. He abolished the Caliphate (rather like abolishing the Vatican); installed a Western-style secular republic; prohibited the wearing of the *fez*; made English the official second language; introduced mass education; emancipated women; changed the written language from Arabic characters to the Roman alphabet; and, most extraordinarily, inspired the army to defend the new order and the constitution, rather than seek power for its own sake as is the habit of many armies. Ataturk was an anything-but-perfect man, as any reader of a fair biography will tell you, but what he did for Turkey catapulted the country from the past to modernity with amazing speed.

We stood through the stillness and the sirens for the full two minutes, respectfully in awe of this demonstration of national fervour.

There was, however, something vaguely troubling about this almost-adoration of one human being. Without Ataturk, what did Turkey cling to? If his memory were to fade, would his legacy fade too? Some 68 years after his death, had the European way of life he had introduced solidified into something more significant than his personal inheritance?

Accidentally Istanbul

I pondered yet again what a complex country this is. I realised I was starting to be thoroughly engrossed by its vast contrasts. Soon we would be back sailing into sunshine and moonlight, stormy squalls and boundless waves. I had started dreaming again about sailing and now the dreams were of travelling always onward: arriving in unfamiliar ports, seeing new people, saying good-bye. The boat seemed to fly faster and faster across the waves until our *hellos* and *good-byes* were dizzying things, people blurring into one another, strangers come and gone in an instant. The water and waves were all around, enveloping, so that I no longer needed to breathe air. The boat could swoop below and above the waves, onward and onward.

I've been here too long perhaps, I would think, waking. The dreams seemed more real than the sheets and carpet and Ted always sleeping like a baby. Lying awake, I realised I had started to feel real affection for this culture, its customs, its many kindnesses. Given what was about to happen, it was good that I was prepared.

25

Staying longer

'Guess what!' Ted arrived home as I was walking out the door.

'What? Tell me quickly or I'll miss my bus to work.' I was checking I had my *akbil*, Turkey's universal public transport pass, in my wallet.

'They want me to stay another semester.'

I had my back to my husband and didn't turn, but I breathed out and in again quickly. 'I knew that would happen. Damn—I forgot my phone.'

'You did *not* know.' He was following me around the flat as I searched.

'I did. Here it is.' I picked up my phone and headed for the door.

'What do you think?'

'Fine.' I was at the door now, nodding.

Accidentally Istanbul

'Just like that?'

'Sure.' I waved while closing the door, giggling. 'Let's stay another semester.'

The words had come out by themselves, light-heartedly, almost as though planted by someone else.

I had time to think about it on the bus. It was true that I had suspected the University might ask him to stay. His arrival might have been an experiment, but listening on the sidelines I could tell it had worked out well.

Why did I agree so flippantly? I could feel the prickle of an adrenaline flow in my chest. It meant that our 'real life' would have to be put on hold for another four months, until summer. But if we stayed in Istanbul, the friendships I had made could continue, and I would love to finish the year with my English students, who were a constant delight. I sorely missed being able to sail whenever I wanted, but my dreams of sailing were calmer now, light-filled fantasies where the boat and I were one, flying through the sky. Gone were the guilt-filled awakenings and the sickness in my stomach that had so often interrupted earlier nights in Turkey.

There were other enticements. My book club had devised an interesting line-up for the next semester. Perhaps, I thought, there was something I could do to 'go on with life' while we were here? Studying? English literature? Writing? I resolved to see what distance learning opportunities there were with Australian universities.

Accidentally Istanbul

But I was still shocked that I had, so *slippingly off the tongue* committed to another semester.

As Christmas approached we expected that, as a 99 per cent Muslim nation, 25 December would be an ordinary day for Turkey. But again our expectations were mistaken. Christmas decorations started appearing all over Istanbul in the streets and shops. Soon the arcades were full of Santa Clauses, reindeer, elves busily making toys, holly decorations, Christmas trees, sprayed snow on shop windows and mistletoe. Every shopping centre was ablaze. *Silent Night* and *Jingle Bells* blared from every music store.

We were mystified, but gradually came to understand. The Turks, ever-keen for a celebration, were showcasing all the symbols of Christmas, but instead of saying *Happy Christmas* to one another, they said *Happy New Year*.

Christmas Day approached and the pace never altered, working up to a huge celebration on New Year's Eve and New Year's Day. However, something much more momentous was occupying the minds of thinking Turks. On 17 December the Council of the EU had agreed to open entry negotiations for Turkey's membership, for which it had been waiting since as far back as 1963. Now joining seemed imminent.

We read of the intense reactions to this across the European world, among both the political élite and rank-and-file citizens. The latter seemed firmly and sometimes fanatically against the idea. Now appreciating the differences between the European

Accidentally Istanbul

culture that I knew so well and Turkish traditions, I found some of the enthusiasm for joining the EU inexplicable. It almost seemed as shallow as 'modern at any cost'. Discussion and argument raged among our friends, seemingly continuously.

For Christmas Day we were invited to the home of an Australian woman who had married a Turkish man 18 years before. The day was like Christmas Days as pictured on Christmas cards, but denied to us in the hot summers of Australia. A fire burned inside, while the last autumn leaves, orange against stark black branches, flew in a fresh breeze mingling with dustings of snow. Again I found that here in Istanbul I could relive my childhood dreams.

A week later we went to a New Year's Party in a Chinese Restaurant, invited by our dear friends Osman and Diane. It was a lively evening, with the women in their designer best, girls with midriffs on display and lots of brightly-coloured floating feather stoles.

The band was up-tempo, the dance floor never empty and one might have been at a similar party in Sydney except for a few unusual elements. Some of the cool young men on the dance floor who had forgotten to shave that morning were wearing Santa hats. Every now and then the band broke into the ubiquitous *Silent Night* or *Jingle Bells*. *Silent Night* with a jazz tempo had us smiling.

I felt like marching over and correcting both the young men and the band. 'Santa hats are only for Christmas,' or 'You can't

Accidentally Istanbul

perform *Silent Night* on 31st December.' I had a private giggle at the absurdity of it.

I was also a little puzzled at the number of birthdays being celebrated. Waiters carried cakes flaming with candles, blown out with gusto by the recipients while others clapped and sang *Happy Birthday* first in Turkish, then in English, the tune the same.

Then someone explained that they were wishing the *year* a happy birthday!

At the countdown to midnight, out marched a regiment of waiters bearing champagne flutes. It was 10 9 8 7 6 5 4 3 2 1 (*ah, this is familiar*) and the band broke into …

I'll Survive. Yes, that 70s' hit by Gloria Gaynor.

Whatever happened to Auld Lang Syne? I thought indignantly. *What on earth does that feminist song have to do with New Year?*

It was followed by yet another particularly raucous version of *Jingle Bells*, again first in Turkish and then in English. I was laughing so much I was crying to be so gloriously culturally confused—but no one noticed.

The evening went on until breakfast, spurred on by the occasional appearance of a table-dancing belly-dancer with the figure and poise of a ballet star. Even the band's lapses into *Jingle Bells* didn't seem so absurd after all. I laugh even now to think how easily the most ingrained habits of a lifetime can be cast aside.

---

* Another significant event happened that 31st December in Turkey. Six zeros were cut off the currency, meaning that now an Australian dollar was worth one Turkish *lira*, instead of a million.

26

Winter white

In January it began to snow. We watched nearly a metre of soft flakes fall in a mere 24 hours, transforming the world outside into a wild fairyland. Snow pellets raced horizontally past the window and on this cold morning only few dark figures passed, leaning into the wind. It was peak hour but the normally bumper-to-bumper traffic was absent. A car went by every couple of minutes, bumbling along on chains.

Birds flew above in great swooping circles. There were small black birds, seagulls and other unknown varieties. Were they flying to keep warm or did they glory in this new white world? Some fought each other like schoolchildren for bread on the snow. I rushed to the kitchen for some old bread and spread it on our windowsill.

Ted set off to work, but in a couple of hours he was back.

Accidentally Istanbul

'What's wrong?' I rushed to meet him as he was closing the front door.

'Well, that was f!)&()*& strange.' He gave a half-grimace, half-grin and slammed his daily paper down as though he wanted to break the glass table. 'Nobody ever tells you anything in that f)*&^(*&^(*! place.'

He explained over morning coffee.

'When I arrived, the rooms were in darkness. Thinking the snow had held everyone up, I went to my office and started to prepare. After about an hour, with the whole place still deathly quiet, the Dean of the School of Architecture wandered through, and looked at me with a stupid expression on his face.

'"What on earth are you doing here?" he asked.

"I'm preparing my lecture. Everyone is very late. Maybe the snow …?"

"Mr Ted," he had said with great patience, "Mr Ted, when it snows, nobody comes to university or school. They are all closed."

"Oh well then, fine—but someone must have forgotten to let me know."

"They don't have to let you know, Mr Ted. If it snows, you stay at home. That's all."'

Ted gulped his coffee. 'Bloody Turks! Staying home just because it's snowing!'

And snow it did, on and on. The harsh lines of concrete walls, gutters, bitumen roads, fences, rubbish and all the ugly detritus of humans' city existence disappeared before our eyes,

Accidentally Istanbul

replaced by gentle hills and valleys of white, covering streets and footpaths and stairways.

Of the street trees, only the firs seemed totally at home, with shawls of snow decorating each branch. As the snow thickened their branches simply flexed so that it slid off harmlessly. Other trees were not so fortunate, their branches twisted at odd angles, struggling, occasionally failing, to support their new burdens of beauty.

Turkish friends Engin and Nalan, whom we had met while sailing, came to stay while the snow was still falling. They showed us secrets of the city we hadn't known before. We ate delicious mussels in a restaurant that served only mussels. We wandered at night in hidden alleys off Istiklal Caddesi while the huge white flakes descended heavily in the now-windless air. Here late at night where crowds were normally milling and rushing, people were sparse. Anonymous black figures with cold pink cheeks and mischievous smiles were building snowmen. They threw them at one another and at us, so we had to skip around the melee, giggling along with our unknown combatants.

We found a warm and cosy timber-walled restaurant where we shook out our snow-covered coats and enjoyed dinner beside a pot-bellied stove.

The snow melted in about a week, normal for Istanbul. Then it fell again and melted once more. The sky remained a ceiling of white and, between falls, the leafless black trees traced patterns above us against the sky. Nature was in hiding, hibernating.

Accidentally Istanbul

Finally as the weeks passed, there began to be stirrings in the black-and-white winter world around us. Green buds began appearing on the trees. Pigeons nested somewhere outside our bathroom window. I couldn't see them but was always lulled by their cooing.

And then so quickly, it seemed, spring was unfolding on the streets. I had not realised how many peach, plum, cherry and pear trees there were until the blossom started to appear. Soon the streets were awash with colour. There were roses too, and wisteria, poinsettia and many other nameless blossoms strange to our eyes. The warm weather came in waves, two or three days at a time, until one day it was no longer freezing, and we knew that the new season had really arrived.

The vast boulevards became busy with gardeners. One day a fellow bus commuter noticed me craning my neck past her to watch the feverish activity. With typical lack of shyness, she suddenly said in excellent English: 'Three million tulips are planted in Istanbul every spring. It's the national flower of Turkey.'

'Really?' I responded weakly. 'That's interesting. I know they're the national flower of the Netherlands.'

'Ah, but tulips have been cultivated in Turkey for at least 3000 years. They were not discovered by Holland until they became very popular in the seventeenth century.'

Silver-haired, crinkle-faced, with a quiet smile of gentle pride, she had said it with soft authority. I contemplated those 3000

Accidentally Istanbul

years. How trippingly off the tongue she said those words. *How must she feel to have a heritage going back 3000 years?*

My new friend started to talk, sometimes dreamily looking out the window, sometimes glancing quickly at me to see if I was listening. I was rapt.

'The tulip,' she said, 'was originally a wildflower growing in Central Asia, but it was carried across with the nomadic tribes and first cultivated in Turkey around 1000 BC. The root was reputed to be very good for the lungs. The sultans in Ottoman times were very fond of tulips, and kept splendid gardens. I think it was the late sixteenth century when our sultan presented some to a European ambassador who was fascinated by their brilliant colours and elegant shape. He took them to Europe. In Holland in particular they really loved our tulip, and good tulips became very, very precious. They were so precious that sometimes they could cost more than a house. They were used like gold, as currency.'

She smiled. 'But all that is a very long time ago—and my bus-stop is coming. I must go.'

'Thank you,' I said in awe. 'I'll remember what you've told me.' I noticed that she had a walking stick secreted beside her seat. 'It's been nice to talk to you, dear,' she concluded.

'Your English is so good,' I said, not wanting her to leave. 'Have you lived in English-speaking territory?'

'Yes, dear, in the UK. I studied history at Cambridge before returning here to teach. But I'm retired now.'

Accidentally Istanbul

I helped her off the bus and she waved merrily as she walked away, slowly and painfully it seemed. Through such chance meetings were my days made sweet.

27

Visitors

Spring brought another kind of flowering. Tourists started arriving and now we were staying longer, friends from Australia and other places started planning visits. Soon they were trailing through in a continual stream.

Ted's spring brought him another role in life. He became an enthusiastic tour guide, taking control, planning what visitors 'must see', mostly with an admonishment that their stay was too short. Over dinner he would drag out maps and guides, describing the best routes to famous highlights as well as small, charming, secret places.

On the days he was not lecturing he would be up with the dawn, planning the day. He marched his victim-guests for many kilometres around the byways and alleyways of 'his' city. When they tired, he would urge 'just one more corner', and then 'only one more' to see his favourite sights.

Accidentally Istanbul

'We're going to see the Horhor antique building today,' he would announce to his captive audience over breakfast. This antique market in Fatih is very hard to find, and was originally a refuge for artists and antique dealers after the Great Fire of 1981. There are over 200 shops with Turkish, Greek and European antiques, as well as some intriguing artisans' outlets. It is truly a heaven for antique-lovers and almost unknown to ordinary tourists.

Or perhaps he would take them to the Ortakoy Jewellery Fair. Situated in an old village now swallowed by the city, it has an elegant neo-Baroque mosque set on the shores of the Bosphorus, rare in that, while tiny compared with some of the more famous mosques, it features high, expansive windows which refract the changing reflections of the water outside. Most of the jewellery, leatherwork, model boats, textiles and even tiny replicas of notable houses in the streets of Ortakoy are hand-made by the sellers.

'Are you sure that they'll like that?' I would interpose, trying to save them from being dragged out unwillingly.

'Of course,' he would counter, brooking no argument. 'You can't *not* be interested in Horhor. It's seven stories of the most fascinating antiques in the world. And on the way we'll go to that underground shopping mall with the sheepskin-lined denim jackets.'

His enthusiasm grew with each new visitor, not to mention his growing knowledge. If he couldn't answer a question, he would be researching it overnight to find an answer.

Accidentally Istanbul

'You've now done more than a dozen tours of the Hagia Sofia, Ted,' I observed one day. 'Don't you get tired of it?'

'Never. Impossible. It's one of the most wonderful buildings in the world. It has been everything from Greek to Roman to Islamic to a museum. And it was built in 537 AD—that makes it over 1500 years old. It changed the very history of architecture. It was the world's largest religious building for almost 1000 years.'

'OK, I believe you. I believe you! But didn't you say it wasn't in your History of Architecture course at Sydney University?'

'I know, I know—all that shows is just how Anglo-minded Australian universities are.'

For Ted to sound even slightly critical of his beloved university was a surprise to me.

'You really love Istanbul, don't you Ted?' asked a friend one evening, sitting exhausted over a drink back in our apartment.

'I do. I guess I do. It's an astonishing city.'

'Do you miss Australia? Come on—I bet there are all sorts of things you crave ...'

'I can't think of anything, no.'

'Beaches?'

'I never liked beaches.'

'What about the beer?'

'Efes beer here is actually better. I'll take you for a beer tomorrow.'

Our friend wouldn't give up. 'You must miss your friends, surely?'

Accidentally Istanbul

Ted smiled. 'You're all coming to visit us here. We see more of you than we did at home.'

'Don't you miss *anything*?' persisted the friend.

Ted looked at me, wonderingly, and for a moment was speechless.

'Vegemite!' he laughed finally '… and we send for that.'

. . .

It was the end of the evening meal, towards the end of May. We were still at the dining table, our nightly candles burning, glasses of red unfinished. Our conversation had so far been pleasant and innocuous.

'The Dean came to see me today.'

'I thought you saw him every day.'

'Yes, but *he came to see me.*'

I said nothing, waiting, but he didn't continue. I had a premonition just by his body language. So I said: 'I thought he would.'

'What do you mean?'

'He was bound to.' I was concentrating on my glass of Shiraz.

'Is something wrong with your wine?'

I looked up, laughing. 'Yes, there's a fly in it. *No*, of course there's not something wrong with my wine. I just want you to continue the conversation.'

'Which conversation?'

Accidentally Istanbul

'Ted Nobbs, you're completely impossible. Aren't you going to tell me what he came to see you about?'

'You already know.'

'Well, you're pretty transparent.'

'So do you want to?'

'For a year or a semester? What did you agree to?'

'I didn't agree to anything. I said I'd talk to you about it. But I'm sure he would like me to complete the year.'

'And you waited three hours after arriving home to tell me this?'

'I wasn't sure what you'd say.'

'Ted Nobbs, don't be crazy! I would *love* to stay! How fantastic!'

'You would *love* to stay? Really? I thought you were just going along with what I wanted to do.'

'Yes—but I'm a lady and a lady can always change her mind.'

• • •

A second year in Istanbul.

We drifted into the new reality as though it was what we had always intended. As the months went by the summer tourist season moved into full swing and foreigners arrived like locusts from all parts of the world, jamming the roads, raising the prices, making life Hell in the Grand Bazaar. Once-quiet streets rang with a cacophony of many languages: German, Italian,

Accidentally Istanbul

French, Russian, Japanese, Korean—even a few Australian accents.

It could only get worse during the summer school holidays, friends told us. They offered dire warnings about the humidity and the crowds. Istanbul residents took the opportunity to flee to holiday houses, their home country or anywhere *not* the city.

Since we both had a three-month academic break, it was a great opportunity to go sailing.

'Does this mean our life will be thrown off course like the last time?' I asked Ted wryly.

But soon we were on the water again and it was like a song to my ears. *On the water again. On the water again.* Gone were the square and lifeless lines of house and flat and street and office, swapped for the lilting, moving, sparkling world of the sea. Our yacht swished and glided, gently falling and rising like a fish, while below decks was a world of polished teak, brass and cushions, sloping and curving and nestling around our lifestyle. There were no straight man-made lines out here on the open sea, just the chameleon waves, the unruliness of the clouds, the chaos of the stars, the never-ending drama of the cliffs and hills of the Turkish coast.

It was a grand summer.

Sailing the fabled coastline of Turkey was something we once would have thought was a high point in our lives. But as time passed, wisps of the memory of Istanbul's magical spires invaded my daily space. I *missed* it!

Accidentally Istanbul

One incident from that time stays in my mind. We had made friends casually, always so easy to do, with the owners of a little coffee shop in a small fishing village. They had come from the big city of Izmir to live near where we were anchored, to get away from the crowds, traffic and smoggy air.

We asked them how they liked living here in this charming village.

'It's wonderful,' said the wife, 'a slower pace of life, fresh air, good for the children.'

'But there are some disadvantages,' added the husband. 'They don't like foreigners very much.'

I was appalled. 'But people here have been so nice to us! What makes you say that?'

'Oh, we don't mean *you*,' said the wife hastily. 'We mean *us*. We're from Izmir!'

If *they* were foreigners, *we* were so alien we were right off their radar screens. This was a reminder never to forget that no matter how much we might come to love this country, no matter how good our Turkish might be, we could never, ever hope to be anything more than foreign guests.

In spite of this we couldn't wait to get back to our life in Istanbul.

Over the summer I had decided to fill my next year with the luxury of some study to enliven my teaching, and had enrolled in a Masters in Writing and Communication at Deakin University, by distance education.

Accidentally Istanbul

At the beginning of September, we returned to our Istanbul life. I was looking forward to it eagerly and the University was waiting for Ted. But I still had not the slightest inkling of what was in store for us.

28

Ebru

Mornings, when Ted went off to the University, were now filled with my studies in literature, while afternoons and some evenings I taught at the refugee school and Berlitz. Our hearts were light. Now I was enjoying the adventure as much as he.

I was at my desk when the knock came on the door. At first it was soft, tentative, more like a shuffle. Outside I found my dear Gül, her ample figure enveloped in a warm red shawl. With her was our *kapıcı*, whom I now knew as Sevket, stamping nervously from foot to foot. I often saw him, in his black trousers, shirt and woollen waistcoat, raking the garden, sweeping the foyer or planting roses in soft, smelly soil.

I beckoned them in, asking: '*Kahve mu, Cai mu?* (Would you like coffee? Tea?)' Gül was business-like this morning, bustling, on a mission.

Accidentally Istanbul

Laboriously, she conveyed in Turkish simple enough for me to understand that Sevket had a daughter, Ebru, who was 17 and in her last year of school. She wanted to win a scholarship to Bahçeşehir University, the very university where Ted taught. Since English was Turkey's official second language, proficiency was a must for a scholarship. They wanted me to coach Ebru to pass her university entrance examination.

Two nights later the diffident knock was by appointment. Ebru stood stiffly at the door. She was plumply adolescent, tall, with the perfect skin so common in Turkish girls. Her dark shiny hair was cut straight and unattractively and the frames of her glasses were large and black and didn't seem to fit her face. She stood there pushing them up her nose, and continued to push them intermittently while she bent awkwardly to remove her shoes. She was very tense.

We sat at our dining room table. I found in the first few moments that her spoken English was almost non-existent, and soon that she was not at all interested in speaking the language. She simply wanted to pass the examination.

'No, no,' I grinned, 'we must speak!' From then on we spent a couple of hours once, sometimes twice a week, half on oral English and half on grammar. Her focused determination was admirable.

As the weeks and months passed, I realised that I was gaining as much as Ebru from these sessions. I heard about her life and the lives of her friends and family. One day she told me her family history.

Accidentally Istanbul

She had been born in Istanbul, but her parents came from Gümüşhane (Silverhouse), near the Black Sea. 'But that's not all,' she said proudly. 'My family true Turkic people.'

'My family *are* true Turkish people.' Leaving out unnecessary verbs is a common trait of spoken Turkish.

'Yes—my family *are* true Turkic people,' she echoed obediently.

'My father's father's father came long, long ago from Urartu. Have you heard of Urartu? It is called *The Lost Kingdom*.'

Immediately I wanted to hear more, but smiled indulgently. 'Urartu? No.' *Lost Kingdom* sounded like the figment of someone's fertile imagination.

Then Ebru told me the tale of Urartu, sometimes called Ararat, or the Lost Kingdom of Van.

'Over 200,000 years ago, before Adam and Eve…'

I had to interrupt. 'No, Ebru—that's the wrong preposition. You mean *after* Adam and Eve, I think.' This is the way in which we worked; I corrected as we talked. But this time it was I who was mistaken.

'No,' she insisted, 'it was before in time. It was *before* Adam and Eve.'

In her halting English she told me that in this land of hers there existed a being called Van, who had already laboured for 300,000 years for the advancement of the planet. In the place where he lived in Urartu stood the priceless Tree of Life. The Power on High approved the dispatch of humans to settle the

Accidentally Istanbul

planet, and Van laboured with his followers to prepare a garden for the first couple, Adam and Eve, transplanting the Tree of Life into it for their use. It was 37,000 years ago when Adam and Eve were introduced, the story went, and then Van left the planet in the care of humankind.

I hardly knew how to react to this preposterous tale.

But Ebru continued undeterred as I corrected her English. The strangest thing was that the Kingdom of Van, Urartu, unlike others which waxed and waned but were remembered afterwards for their achievements, had been completely forgotten by the world. It was not until the beginning of the twentieth century that historians discovered its existence and stories.

'And this is where you come from?' I hardly knew how to react.

'Yes, I learned these stories from my grandmother.' Ebru's pride seemed to flow like a stream around her body.

'Your parents must be very proud of you, wanting to go to university,' I encouraged her.

'Yes—they were never able to go themselves.'

We worked together for months and at the end of the year Ebru was accepted for university. I was overjoyed at my small part in her success.

The blossoming of young Ebru was in stark contrast to the occasional horrific incident reported in *The Turkish Daily News*.

One story was of a wife and mother of two children, the older a boy of 14. Continually beaten by her husband, she ran away from her village in eastern Turkey to relatives in Istanbul, who welcomed her. The husband's family, however, assured her that if she went home, the husband would beat her no more. After several months of persuasion, she agreed to return. When she arrived and alighted from the bus, the husband and her two children were there waiting. The 14-year-old son produced a gun and shot his mother dead.

Our friends explained to us, tight-lipped, that the eldest son, still a minor, would have been persuaded to kill his mother to restore the honour of the family. Because of his age he would escape severe punishment and, they thought, be praised by the people of his village.

We read that the Turkish government was trying hard to eliminate such 'honour killings'. It had enacted a sweeping human rights law that abolished a provision that used to reduce prison terms for crimes of 'family honour'.

When we heard of such incidents, recounted with relish by the newspapers, the stories had the quality of nightmares. When I thought of the rich, gentle atmosphere of Istanbul, with its many successful professional women and its universities full of upwardly-mobile young women, whose comparative freedom of choice was written all over their beaming faces, I found the other sad, horrific tales difficult to believe, much less understand. I recalled the time we had spent while sailing near coastal villages and found it even harder to relate such stories to those we had met.

But Istanbul, as I was repeatedly reminded by Turkish and experienced Western friends alike, is *not* Turkey.

Accidentally Istanbul

And what happened afterwards to Ebru? She graduated from Bahçeşehir University with flying colours and found a good position in a freight forwarding company. She grew her hair, rid herself of her spectacles and some kilos, and became the beautiful young swan she was always destined to be.

Much later, my niece, a marketing executive with Emirates, met with Ebru and me on a fleeting working visit to Istanbul. Through a lunch-time conversation, Ebru was encouraged to seek employment with an airline so that she could see the world outside Turkey. She applied to Turkish Airlines to work as a flight attendant, but was refused because of a mild problem with her sight. I urged her not to give up, suggesting she try other airlines. Instead, with typical determination, she cheekily wrote letters to both the CEO of Turkish Airlines and the Turkish Minister for Aviation, presenting her case.

This worked. Ebru is now a gorgeous and well-travelled young woman, married but still flying to all corners of the world, after graduating from domestic to international flights. Ted and I continue to follow her life with the greatest interest.

29

The test

I thought I was becoming used to the unexpected in Istanbul, but never could have anticipated the next surprise. My daughter Kassandra, a working sculptor in Sydney, was to visit us. I had an older friend who was a tour guide, and with typical Turkish kindness he offered to take her one morning around the Istanbul art scene, introducing her to some of his artist friends.

When Kassandra returned that evening she seemed to be breathing very lightly and greeted us in a preoccupied way. Since she had been suffering from flu, I was worried.

'Are you feeling all right?' I asked her once we were alone.

'No', she said, but with a curious half-smile, pushing her luxuriously curly, dark hair away from her face. 'I'm not. I found that sculptor I met very interesting. And he'—short intake of air—'he finds me interesting too.'

Accidentally Istanbul

In all my years of listening to the stories of Kassandra's love life, I had never heard her talk with such breathless reserve. She had enjoyed some great affairs of the heart and discarded many lovers, but never married. Very attractive, she always had a steady stream of men at her beck and call. As a mother I was always vitally interested.

'But I thought Mustafa said before you left that the sculptor you were visiting couldn't speak English?'

'No, he can't really—or not much. But he's so ... communicative ... and ... talented. He has such noble ideas—and a very curious mind. You should see his work. It's amazing.'

Just then her mobile phone rang. By the instant change of expression, a quick half-smile and intake of breath, I could tell it was *the sculptor*. She began to speak in very simple English, flushed and concentrating very hard. I had ceased to exist.

So the romance began. His name was Cemil (pronounced Jameel).

She took us to meet Cemil at his studio. She had told us that he was unveiling a new work, *The Dancing Man* and wanted us to share this with him. 'It would be a good way to meet him,' she said.

We travelled to Kadikoy on the Asian side of Istanbul, accompanied by a friend, Arzu, who could translate if necessary. I think I was more nervous than if it were my own new love I was about to meet.

I could see immediately why Kassandra was attracted to

Accidentally Istanbul

Cemil. It was his hands that I noticed first: white, muscular, soft, moving, like a dancing echo of his words. Then his words: strong, measured, thoughtful. And his eyes were a surprising blue, intense and searching. He had a face that seemed all angles and a billowing torrent of light brown hair to his shoulders. As he spoke, nothing seemed still. His voice was soft yet vehement, hesitating as he searched for words in English to express his meaning.

The ceiling of his studio was high and painted a harsh white. Skylights threw angled light across the delicate forms of the many sculptures lining the walls in haphazard profusion. Dust motes flew in the sunshine as he talked on and on, passionate. I gazed at his sculptures, their fluid shapes seeming to move and dance despite their stillness.

Pictures of some of his previous works were pasted to the studio walls, with cuttings from some of Turkey's leading newspapers such as *Cumhurriet*, *Sabah* and *The Turkish Daily News*. The cuttings told me he was one of the most promising young sculptors in Turkey. The tall figure that we assumed was the new work remained swathed in plastic, alone in the middle of the open space. We were too polite to ask about it.

It was chic, this studio. It could have been in any of the great metropolises: Paris, New York, London. Yet here we were in Kadikoy, on the Asian side of Istanbul. In one corner, a nest of elegant old furniture stood around a pot-bellied stove. Every surface was covered with clay dust, charcoal, dog-eared paper

Accidentally Istanbul

sketches, pens, pencils and brushes, and on its rough floor pools of paint had been spilled, bright against the white walls.

This young man who had so impressed my daughter was trying in his musical accented English to frame a delicate thought. The words that finally became clear were: he was broke.

Broke? With all the success and fame described in the articles? With so many commissions throughout Turkey to his credit? What about all these rave reviews on the walls?

'Well, you see—' He paused, carefully choosing his words, allowing Arzu to translate when he stumbled, 'two things happened in Turkey in the last few years. First there was the economic crash of 2001, and that meant no private commissions. Then the government changed, and the new conservatives had other things on their minds, so funding for art dried up.'

He went on to explain that the tradition of 'art works' in the Western sense of the word was a relatively new concept in Turkey.

Speaking softly but intensely, he outlined how modern Turkish art and sculpture had developed. Depiction of the human body went into long hibernation during the dominance of Islam over the 1300 years of the Ottoman Empire. Conservative Islam frowns on such representation as being the proper work of God, not man. When Ataturk separated the functions of mosque and state in 1923, this allowed the flowering of freedom of expression not seen since the Byzantine

Accidentally Istanbul

era ended. The tradition of which Cemil was part, he explained, was only 83 years old, the age of the Republic.

I pondered his words. It was unsurprising that the new Parliament dominated by a conservative party would have little enthusiasm for art works contrary to traditional Islamic teachings. But in spite of this, Cemil had large sculptures in public places spread across Turkey, from Istanbul in the far west to Tonya in the northeast. He worked in bronze and marble and wax, and made ceramics and his forms were, inevitably it seemed, human.

'I've come a long way from my childhood', he said. 'In my village, no one has ever worked as a sculptor. It was strange for them.' His was a Pontic family from the northeast, people famous for their music and dancing. Their rich traditions, he explained, reached further than Turkey, into Greece, the old Yugoslavia and across the Middle East to Iran and Uzbekistan.

'My parents had no connection with sculpture—and they didn't understand what I was doing. But my father never forced me to change. He was very special, a musician. I'm talented musically too. If I didn't have sculpture, I would have been a musician. Sometimes I think I have too many abilities.'

At the age of eight, his art teacher had become his mentor, encouraging and inspiring him. 'I fell in love with her,' he said, his face creasing in smiles. 'I still talk to her. She phones to congratulate me if she reads in the newspaper that I've won a prize.'

I laughed with him. 'Are you still in love with her?'

Accidentally Istanbul

He hesitated. 'Oh no. well yes ...' Now he was all charm. 'There's a separate shelf in my life for each of my loves.'

I was still very conscious of the tall swathed figure dominating the studio. The local government in Trabzon had commissioned Cemil to create a statue of a traditional musician from the area. This was a great personal triumph for him. His hometown was acknowledging the success of one of its sons.

The figure was towering, maybe three metres high, and draped in fine milky plastic. Finally the time came for its unveiling. I was fascinated by Cemil's reverence, the loving way he removed the wrappings. We were silent, watching—I a little breathless—as the figure emerged from its shroud. It was still wet. Ochre-coloured, the dancer was dressed in pantaloons and a vest and was playing the *kemençe*, a small stringed instrument. He loomed above us.

It was the face that was riveting: a big swooping jaw below a large nose and deep-set eyes that shone with intelligence and humour. He was dancing and playing his instrument at the same time, his attention focused on his music but his eyes soft with the pleasure he was sharing with his audience.

At last I could understand the magic in the hands of this young man now kneeling humbly at the foot of his masterpiece, *The Dancing Man*.

Within a week Kassandra and Cemil were inseparable. Within two weeks they were engaged.

Kassandra broke the news in an intimate way, sharing coffee

in the kitchen. As always when she talked of Cemil, there was that air of barely-suppressed excitement about her.

I had been ready for anything when she broke the news that he had proposed.

'Really? After a week?'

'It's two weeks.'

'Oh well, right—so it is. And?'

'And I accepted.'

We hugged and kissed and Kassandra giggled and cried and we were both overcome with the moment.

I could hardly take it in. It seemed only yesterday that Ted and I had arrived to have a short sailing holiday along the coast of Turkey. And now we were to have a Turkish son-in-law! Cemil and Ted, the artist and the architect, found they had much to talk about. I found him the most charming of young men.

What followed was a complex, many-sided love affair between the two sculptors as they came to know one another intimately. After a couple of weeks Kassandra was taken to Trabzon to meet the family. This must have been shock for them, since in all his 37 years he had never taken a girlfriend home.

Kassandra's phone calls from Trabzon oscillated between joy and uncertainty. Although considered among the gentry of the Pontic people, Cemil's family life seemed dominated by the growing of vegetables which they then shared and swapped with neighbours. Kassandra was embraced whole-heartedly and became very close to Cemil's mother, who donned a headscarf

Accidentally Istanbul

when she went out to work in her vegetable garden.

My daughter reported that within this Turkish family everyone talked at once and no one listened. This she quite enjoyed, but the constant presence of others and the lack of privacy were hard to take. She waxed hot, then cold. The lavishness of Cemil's affection she found claustrophobic at times but at others heavenly.

While Cemil waited for a visa to visit Australia, Kassandra flew back and forth between the two countries, balancing her work commitments with her desire to further the relationship.

While she was in Australia we spent lengthy periods with our son-in-law-to-be. Ted and Cemil had much in common: archaeology and architecture and the philosophy of art, today and yesterday.

Kassandra came and went. I found myself making plans for the wedding, glorying in my new-found status as Turkish mother-in-law. We were no longer mere tourists or temporary workers but had a permanent connection with the country we had accidently discovered. I spread the news around all my friends and contacts in Istanbul with the greatest delight. My own connection with Istanbul, with the Bosphorus and its seagulls, with the age-old streets and the myths and legends that were so much part of my childhood, were now mine to own, even if in an indirect way.

Before they made a firm date for the wedding, Kassandra wanted Cemil to see Australia. While she was happy to stay, even

Accidentally Istanbul

live in Istanbul, she knew that her home town would always be special and she wanted Cemil to see it with her. As the weeks and months went by we waited in vain for Cemil's visa, notoriously difficult to obtain for single Turkish men. Kassandra and he marked time in Istanbul, enjoying one another's company whenever she could spare the time to visit between her commissions.

The end came as suddenly as it had begun.

'I went for a walk,' said Kassandra. 'I told Cemil that was what I was doing. I was away about two hours. When I got back, he was frantic.'

'Where on earth were you?' he had shouted. 'You said you were going for a walk. Why were you away so long? Why do you want to walk without me?'

'I was only *walking*,' she said forlornly. 'That's what I told him.'

She also described doing the chores. 'I say: "I'll vacuum the flat." He says: "Good. I was thinking of doing that—so I'll help you." I say: "No, two of us can't do it. If you want to vacuum the flat, you do that and I'll make some soup." He says: "I want to help you make the soup." He doesn't get it. His culture is too different—and so are his expectations.'

She took a deep breath. 'We can't make it together. I'm sorry. I'm going home.'

Of course, this break-up wasn't all about walks, soup and vacuum cleaners. I was sad—but their lives were their own to live.

So Kassandra went back to Australia and another chapter in

Accidentally Istanbul

our lives passed. On our way home from the airport to see her off, tears welled up before I knew how disappointed I was.

'Sorry to see her go?' Ted was always good at stating the obvious.

'It's not that. For a moment I thought that we could have a *real* connection with Istanbul.'

'A real connection?'

'You know—a permanent one.'

'I thought I dragged you here.'

'Yes, you did. That's true.'

He grinned and clasped my hand, looking tactfully out the window to allow me my time to be sad.

I went on being sad for longer than was reasonable. For weeks I carried an inexplicable bleakness through all my days. I was grieving—but not for my daughter, who was back in Australia and happy with her life. The solution was there, a way to rid myself of the cheerlessness hanging around me like a dark cloak—but I didn't want to acknowledge it. It took some time but, finally, when I came to admit the truth to myself, it seemed so obvious it was like headlights coming towards you on a country road at night.

30

Dilemmas

In spite of my continuing sadness at the end of Kassandra's relationship, this was a rich time for Ted and me in Istanbul. I was enjoying studying, teaching and, in free times, exploring the sights and the rest of Turkey. Our lives, which had begun so uncertainly in this great city, were now more stimulating and busy than I could ever have imagined.

Nevertheless, my sadness at the loss of a permanent connection with the country persisted. Conflicted as I was, I wanted to witness the changing face of Turkey and its acceptance or otherwise into the EU, and also to continue our pleasant daily lives. In private moments at the dead of night, with Ted's calm contented breathing beside me, niggling thoughts would still keep me awake. I acknowledged how superior I had felt when we arrived. This had been replaced by guilt that I had

Accidentally Istanbul

been so arrogant when kindness and friendliness had constantly welcomed me.

In the morning these dark thoughts would evaporate into the bliss of my days. I said nothing to Ted. I knew he could tell how much I was beginning to love this country. Kassandra's short-lived romance had been a turning point for me, and made me tell myself the truth: I now loved Istanbul. Ted floated easily through his days and I knew I was becoming more deeply involved with the community, and constantly stimulated by the environment, passionately involved in the developing political situation, fascinated by the beauty of the place and even its flaws: totally immersed.

We lived through a second winter enjoying the occasional snow which paralysed the city but gave us unexpected holidays. By this time it seemed normal that an electrician might finish his job and set about repairing our plumbing, or that the bazaar vendor should slip in a couple of free tomatoes with the bananas. Now I always tried to purchase small things from street sellers, knowing that they had families proud of their efforts.

I was no longer surprised that the footpaths were so uneven, knowing how ancient the streets were, or worried that they were littered with cat bowls full of food, or a hundred other things that had seemed so strange.

As summer approached it marked the end of our official time in Turkey. The knowledge that we would soon be gone caused a small ache in my chest. *How different our departure would have*

Accidentally Istanbul

been had we left a daughter and son-in-law behind us. I began to cherish every detail of the stimulation of the vibrant city around us, missing it even while we were still there.

I imagined Turkey in my reveries as a Goliath standing, hands on hips, astride the great waterway that divided East and West. I wondered whether Ted was also experiencing sadness at the approaching end of our adventure. I knew he had never stopped loving the great street-scapes of wonderful buildings that infused him with such joy and put a spring in his step. Occasionally now as we walked he would draw me to him in an almighty hug, and I understood that he was lost for words to describe just how happy he was to be walking in *this* street, at *this* moment, with *me*.

I was going to miss the tolerant-to-all-religions culture in the society around us. I couldn't help remembering the anti-Muslim sentiments of some Australians. I had come to love the friends we had made, both Turkish and foreigners, and the free-wheeling discussions we had about politics and religion, pollution and population, the future of the world in our hands, propelled by an abundant media expressing the widest possible range of views.

Leaving Australia had, for me, been like a teenager leaving Mum and Dad to explore the world. It was a rite of passage. One left with the knowledge that home would always be waiting. Leaving Istanbul would be more like leaving a sweet love affair, with the stabbing pain of a romantic love lost. Nothing would ever be the same.

Accidentally Istanbul

The sights and sounds of the city echoed through my reveries as if I had already left: the *Ezan*, the Call to Prayer, achingly beautiful as it echoed around the seven hills of Istanbul, reminding me as it swelled in my chest and vibrated in the air, penetrating some indefinable part of me that was neither body nor mind, of the inevitable and steady passage of the seasons. I pictured the seagulls over the Galata Bridge, fishermen jostling, ships in the salt-mist as they marched their cargoes down the fast-flowing waterway between Asia and Europe. The practicality of these fishermen, heads bent to their tasks, impressed me. They would provide the next family meal. Images flashed into my head of a narrow back-street with children playing and old men chatting, watching over them. I felt the warmth and simple kindness I felt every day as I moved around the city. No matter where I lost my wallet or my umbrella it would always be waiting for me when I returned. I thought how inspired I was by the complexity of Turkey's political challenges and the bright optimism of its young people.

I loved the way the ancient cobblestones echoed the ghostly footsteps of the millions of people who had walked where I now walked and created the fairy tales and myths that had been a part of my childhood, so that my imaginary world had been so different from the rock and shale of the footpaths I walked to school. Now as I rambled in Istanbul, dreamed, talked, slept, it seemed as though there was an expanding bubble of air inside my chest, making me lighter. I felt illuminated by the lightness

Accidentally Istanbul

of the city. Its magic would remain after we left, for others.

Then, as the days passed, there was a single thought that began to arrive at unexpected times, in daylight, in small lightning strikes, small terror-attacks so sharp and frightening that they would ricochet off and away, only to return in the dead of night, crashing down into my dreams. Awakened, I would stare at the invisible ceiling, roll and toss in a tangle of sheets, unsure whether it was the dazzle or the fear that kept me from sleep.

Weeks passed and we commenced arranging our farewells. So many friends. So much to lose.

In the end, it came to me suddenly.

'Ted—' I was breathing shallowly, the air trembling in my throat.

'Mmmm.' He was reading *The Turkish Daily News,* sitting in the after-breakfast sunshine streaming through the window. Soon he would be up and away to the University and I would return to my desk and my studies.

'We could buy an apartment.' It was almost a whisper.

'Now Erdoğan is denying that he wants to be President—'

'Ted.'

'Yes.' *I'm busy reading and I don't have much time—*

Louder. 'We could buy an apartment.'

'Where?'

'We could buy an apartment here in Istanbul.'

Now I now had his attention. He looked up slowly from his newspaper, rustling it on to his knees.

Accidentally Istanbul

'What for?'

'We could come back after we've been home to see the families.'

'Come back? What for?'

'I'm not sure—but do we really have to give up our life here? Isn't there some way we can extend it?'

Now he sat up straight in his chair and took his glasses off. 'What are you saying?'

'You heard what I said.'

'Are you crazy? We can't *stay* here!'

'We're the only ones who have to decide.'

'You mean *live* here?'

'Well, at least for some of the year. If we buy something, we have a link. It would be easy to come back and live here as long as we liked, when we chose.'

'But you don't even like it here—or you didn't. This was just an adventure, Nance, an opportunity. Nothing else. You simply can't be serious.'

I hadn't anticipated this degree of shock and rejection. As I turned to look out the window, my chest caved in, without breath. My voice, when it came, was small in my throat, with little air to push it forward. I wasn't even sure whether I said this, or merely thought it: 'Oh, I thought you might like the idea—'

It has to be both of us who want to stay, not just me.

Over the road on the vacant sportsfield and the Boğaziçi

Accidentally Istanbul

Universitesi Spor Tesisleri, seagulls from the Bosphorus were gathering on the grass, skittering about, squawking, landing in waves. 'It's going to blow,' I said. 'The seagulls are coming in.' I had controlled the catch I felt in my voice. Instead I watched the birds alighting on the vacant field, squabbling among themselves. Even this scene brought another small stab of anguish. Once we left, I would never again see it.

An old woman, a little bent and with a long pale coat and a dark headscarf stood with her back to us, watching the gulls with me, but in her case through the fence. I recognised her. It was our flower seller. She reached into her bag and drew out something from its depths, crumbs maybe, and threw them through the fence.

Ted's voice murmured behind me. 'Like the idea! Like the idea?' He seemed to be talking to himself. I turned slowly

'You do or you don't?'

There was the hint of amusement playing around his mouth. 'Would you really want to do that? I've always thought you were only trying to make the best of this for my sake.'

'In the beginning maybe—but not now.'

'Do you remember how resistant you were? Remember the conversations about *those Muslims?*"

I said nothing. There seemed little to say.

He leant back in his chair and stared out the window, over the distant skyline of the city. His newspaper was forgotten; his brow furrowed as he contemplated all possible obstacles.

Accidentally Istanbul

'What about—?' he began ...

That evening, we sat far into the night talking, dreaming, examining. But there was no further discussion about whether or not we would actually do what I had suggested. It was as if it had been decided during the day, while we were absent from one another.

In the days that followed we talked only about where we would live and how much we would pay for an apartment. I carried a feeling of breathless unreality with me as we spoke, which only increased as we started to look at actual places. I told no-one, not my friends in Istanbul nor even my family at home, for fear that it would break some spell that I must be under. After several weeks of searching we found somewhere within our budget just off Istiklal Caddesi. We bought it.

The other owners in the building were traditionally Turkish. Our next-door neighbour was a quiet, soft woman who still leant out the window to send down her shopping basket containing money on a long rope. Roving street vendors would fill it with bread or vegetables from the carts they rolled round the back streets. Inside, our apartment was crisp and modern. Outside the Call to Prayer competed with church bells to serenade us in the mornings.

What, exactly, is Islamophobia? Is that the affliction I had suffered when I arrived in Istanbul? Or was it merely a Westerner's arrogant assumption that we know and do everything better? I tried hard to remember exactly why I had

Accidentally Istanbul

resisted the idea of spending time in Istanbul. But while I could recall incidents, I couldn't remember, and still can't, the soul of who I was then.

Could life continue in this new and kinder way we had found? One never knew, but if we didn't reach out for it, the dream might fly out of our reach and blow away in the afternoon breeze.

We would certainly head for home when the semester ended, back to where family and children were waiting. But we had decided that life should be lived the way you dream, and, even if it was accidentally, we had found a new life with meaning, with depth, aspiration and fulfilment.

In Istanbul.

Epilogue

The events of this story happened in 2004-06. The Global Financial Crisis, which made us all realise there are no economic islands left in the world, was still to come. The death of Osama bin Laden, which we all hoped might end the power of Al Qaeda, did not stop the rise of fanatical fundamentalist Islam. The hundreds of millions of people in the Muslim world had not yet been caught in the spotlight of Western paranoia and xenophobia, shocked, like rabbits in the headlights. We were still to realise the full import of world-wide instant communication through IT devices, of the mixing-pot world that easy global travel gave us, or how everything, just everything, would soon happen in your living room and could no longer be seen as 'over there'.

Once we were set on our path there was no looking back, and neither of us faltered for a moment. We went back to Australia and have since returned to Istanbul for part of every year. With

Accidentally Istanbul

all our family in Australia, we now have allegiances in both countries and see the jewels and flaws of both. Both Christian and Jewish friends continue to question our love for Turkey, and we spend much time on a small two-man crusade to undo what the original Crusades seemed so effectively to achieve all those hundreds of years ago: to hard-wire a mistrust of Islam even in the minds of declared atheists. At the time of writing, the struggle goes on, and we are still continually explaining it to ourselves.

Acknowledgements

Heartfelt thanks go to my long-time editor Diana Giese for her untiring support, guidance, and unfailing enthusiasm during the editing and production process in turning my manuscript into a publishable book.

Thanks to Audrey Larsen for her patience and dedication to creating a great and meaningful design.

I would like to acknowledge my friend and fellow Istanbul-based writer, Lesley Tahtilic, for her willingness to check my facts and language.

Thanks also to all those people who made the book possible by being part of my life: Cemil, Ebru, Gŭl, Şerefe, Ali, Fehmi, Osman and Diane, Claudia and T, Malcolm and Carolyn and my daughter Kassandra, and to the many other anonymous people who inhabit this book and so eminently figure in my story, for their generosity of heart and their inspiration—the origin of this narrative.

Finally to my husband and best buddy Ted Nobbs for his continuing confidence, encouragement and again, patience.

www.ingramcontent.com/pod-product-compliance
Lightning Source LLC
Chambersburg PA
CBHW020612300426
44113CB00007B/608